Introduction to Database Systems Modeling and Administration

James M. Reneau Ph.D.

Technics Publications, LLC
115 Linda Vista,
Sedona, AZ 86336 USA

https://www.TechnicsPub.com

Edited by Steve Hoberman

Cover design by Lorena Molinari

First Printing 2025 (2025-03-23 22:22:37)

ISBN, print ed.	9781634627269
ISBN, Kindle ed.	9781634627276
ISBN, PDF ed.	9781634627283

Acknowledgments

No work like this stands on its own. I would have been unable to write this without the years of working with my clients, the hundreds of students in my classes at Shawnee State University, the educators who gave to me their time and knowledge, the open source community for all of the really amazing tools, and the support of my loving wife and family.

Special acknowledgement goes out to:

- Ms. V. Jayne - My first real writing instructor.
- Ms. E. Jayne - Who taught me to love mathematics.
- Dr. W. Rodgers - My first database professor at Morehead State University.
- Mr. S. Biros - My second database instructor at Marshall University.
- Dr. J. Sun - My third database professor at Nova Southeastern University.
- Mr. R. Pick - For creating the PICK database.
- Mr. S. Hoberman - For his great texts on data modeling and support.
- Mrs. N. Tresch-Reneau - My long suffering wife and biggest cheerleader.

Software

Databases and Versions

- MySQL and MariaDB
  - MariaDB - Server version: 11.4.3-MariaDB-1
- SQLite
  - Version 3.46.1
- MSSQL Server
  - Microsoft SQL Server 2022 (RTM-CU16) (KB5048033) - 16.0.4165.4 (X64)

Writing Tools

- OS
  - Ubuntu 24.10 workstations.
- Editing
  - Ghostwriter - Version 25.07.70 - Edit the Markdown and Latex files.
  - Geany - Version 2.0 - Edit the SQL, Python, and bash script files.
  - Draw.io - Version 26.0.9 - ORM2 Diagrams, IE (crows foot) ERDs, and Relational diagrams.
  - Inkscape - Version 1.2 - Other line art.
  - LanguageTool -Version 6.6-SNAPSHOT - Spelling and grammar checker.
- Document rendering
  - Pandoc - Version 3.5 - Markdown to Latex and ePub.
  - pdfTeX - Version 3.141592653-2.6-1.40.26 - Rendering Latex to PDF.
  - Python - Version 3.12.
  - Custom Python scripting by author.

Companion Web Site

You can find more resources at http://www/learn2db.com, or by scanning the QR code below.

This page intentionally left blank.

Contents

This page intentionally left blank.

Introduction

This book is an introduction to data modeling and Structured Query Language (SQL). It is intended for an undergraduate introduction to database systems course. Additionally the learning outcomes specified in the Ohio Department of Higher Education's Transfer Acceptance Guide (TAG) for the course OIS001-INTRODUCTION TO DATABASE ADMINISTRATION/MANAGEMENT have fully been covered.[1] The modeling techniques are based upon the recommendations made in the *DAMA-DMBOK Data Managers Body of Knowledge*.[2]

SQL Variants Covered

MySQL, MariaDB, SQLite, and MSSQL Server will be covered in the SQL chapters. For some chapters and statements, the variations are minor and the statement syntax will be displayed in a table with icons for the variants. If the differences are significant between databases, there may be sections or subsections with their own examples and discussion. Statements without a notation have been tested and work in all three.

MySQL and MariaDB

MySQL variant of statement, function, or output. This should also apply to the open source MariaDB loaded by default on many LINUX systems.

SQLite

SQLite variant of statement, function, or output.

MSSQL Server

Microsoft's SQL Server (written as 'MSSQL Server') variant of statement, function, or output.

---

[1]Ohio Department of Higher Education. (2023). OIS001- INTRODUCTION TO DATABASE ADMINISTRATION/MANAGEMENT. Retrieved from https://tinyurl.com/bddrawah

[2]Henderson, D., Earley, S., & Bradley, C. (2024). Dama-DMBOK: Data Management Body of Knowledge. Technics Publications. https://www.dama.org/cpages/body-of-knowledge

This page intentionally left blank.

Chapter 1 - What is a Model and Why Model Data?

This chapter will discuss why humans have created models of complex things and situations. People have been drawing diagrams about hunting and carving representations of ourselves and the world around us for millennia. Data is no different. An organization's data and information needs are extremely complex and can be almost impossible to understand without modeling.

Objectives

At the conclusion of this lesson module, students will be able to:

1. describe the differences between data, information, and knowledge.
2. define a data model.

Modeling

Humans have been creating models and diagrams representing complex situations since before we had a formal written language. Cave paintings of food animals from a Borneo cave have been discovered dating back 40,000 to 52,000 years.[3] [4]

---

[3]https://www.nytimes.com/2018/11/07/science/oldest-cave-art-borneo.html)
[4]https://commons.wikimedia.org/w/index.php?curid=74274155

Figure 1: Photo by Luc-Henri Fage, www.fage.fr

Carvings and clay figurines of animals and the hunt have a history going back as far or further than the cave paintings. What were these ancestors of ours doing? They were modeling.

The Merriam-Webster dictionary has several different definitions of a **model** but the one that applies in this context is "a description or analogy used to help visualize something (such as an atom) that cannot be directly observed".[5]

We use models to gain an understanding of complex systems that we cannot fully understand.

An architect creates several different models of a building before it is finally constructed. These include simple sketches, building with cardboard, 3-D computer models that allow a client to walk through a virtual building, and the final plans that show the location of wires and ducts inside the walls. Each of these models have a different level of accuracy, or fidelity, and are created for a specific purpose.

Imagine you are going to model an airplane. A low-fidelity model might be

---

[5]https://www.merriam-webster.com/dictionary/model

a paper airplane that will fly but does not look like the final real-world item. Another low-fidelity model might be a small hand held plastic model of the same plane. It will not fly, but it looks much more like the real thing. A higher-fidelity and larger radio-controlled (RC) model will fly and look like the final plane but the cargo, seating, and final construction details will be missing. The manufacturer will even build large models for testing in a wind tunnel and full size models of specific features.

Each model, of usually increasing fidelity, is used to gain insight into the complex and to make sure that we don't miss anything important in our build.

What is Data?

Data is "factual information (such as measurements or statistics) used as a basis for reasoning, discussion, or calculation" according to the Merriam-Webster dictionary.[6] Data fall into four major categories: 1) categorical, 2) resource, 3) event/transaction, and 4) event/transaction detail. The four categories of data entities will be discussed in detail in the chapter on entities.

Data, Information, and Knowledge

So we can think of **data** as the temporal and transactional facts that are collected in the operation of a business or system. These facts can be voluminous. In fact, there can be so many with such detail that the human mind would be unable to comprehend what all the facts mean.

Information is the product of summarizing the detail transaction data, the event data, and sometimes the reference data into counts and totals by dates, date ranges, individual reference data items, groups of reference items, and by categorical data items. To simplify, information is distilled data (usually totals and counts) that are meaningful to individuals. For example, the general ledger transaction data that contains debits and credits to specific accounts in specific periods is summarized into meaningful financial reports like a Trial Balance or Profit and Loss Statement.

Knowledge is when information is internalized by a user and used to get an insight into what is happening. When a leader gets the report (information), they use it to make quality decisions. We can say that they have gained knowledge from the raw data.

What is a Data Model?

Data, especially for an enterprise or a difficult problem, can be very complex. Like an architect who is designing a large building starts with a few simple diagrams. Data modelers also use diagrams to gain insight into the real problem and all the data needed to be collected.

---

[6]https://www.merriam-webster.com/dictionary/data

A data model:

- describes a system's data, and it does not contain actual data.
- is usually graphical and as concise as possible.
- is used to communicate to stakeholders and technical people how the entities, attributes, and relationships within the data work together.

Data models also have the following characteristics:

- Incremental - A data model is built in a process that grows in detail. Often one piece at a time.
- Iterative - A data model is a living document that will grow and change as requirements are discovered and maintenance is completed.
- Collaborative - It can only be created through open communication with stakeholders, managers, internal and external subject matter experts, analysts, and database administrators. It cannot be created in a vacuum.

Data models do not contain the data or samples of the data but contain descriptions about the data. The descriptions may include the type of data, the domain of data elements (range), cardinality (count) of elements and occurrences, and names to go with elements of the model. We call data about data, metadata.

Data models are usually graphical. There is an old adage that a "picture is worth a thousand words" and when it comes to a data model it is often many more. As each data model gains fidelity and gets closer to the physical implementation of the database, the diagram becomes more complex.

Fidelities of Data Models

We usually speak of data models on four increasing levels of complexity:

1. the Enterprise Data Model (EDM),
2. the Conceptual Data Model (CDM),
3. the Logical Data Model (LDM), and
4. the Physical Data Model (PDM).

This text will primarily focus on the middle two, the CDM and the LDM.

Enterprise Data Model (EDM)

The Enterprise Data Model (EDM) is a model of the various applications or systems in a company and how these systems relate and share data at a high level.[7] This essential part of creating an enterprise architecture is a map of how data is used, organised, and stored.

An EDM may exist in many different fidelities, from a conceptual view of the major systems and their data flows to a physical view with all of the data tables and stores in a variety of databases and systems.

---

[7] https://www.ewsolutions.com/common-components-of-an-enterprise-data-model/

Conceptual Data Model (CDM)

The Conceptual Data Model (CDM) is a diagram of entities with relationships between them. Much of the detail seen in later diagrams is left out, intentionally. It is to get a high level understanding of what data needs collecting and how it all connects. In this book, we will be using a simplified version of the **Object-Role Model 2** (ORM2) type of diagram to draw these models.[8]

Logical Data Model (LDM)

The Logical Data Model (LDM) includes entities, relationships, and the important attributes of entities. It is how we think about the data and is used to validate and make sure that our model will work within the business requirements. It also is used as a tool so that everybody involved in the project has a clear understanding of the data. These will be drawn as simple Information Engineering (IE) style Entity Relationship Diagram (ERD) in this text. Some authors and data modelers use the Chen Notation for drawing ERDs.[9]

Physical Data Model (PDM)

The most detailed model is the Physical Data Model (PDM). It represents how the data is actually implemented on the relational database. All attributes, keys, foreign keys, relationships, and data types are defined on this diagram. Programmers and data analysts will often have this diagram posted on their wall, or at least handy, so that they know where to look for data and how to connect entities. The data is usually in third normal form (3NF) or better.[10]

Exercises

1. In your own words, define data, information, and knowledge. Use the book and external resources.
2. All data models have three common attributes. List and define in your own words.
3. Data models usually are categorized into one of three levels of complexity. Define these levels and describe them.

---

[8]http://www.orm.net/pdf/EncDBS.pdf

[9]https://support.microsoft.com/en-us/office/create-a-diagram-with-chen-s-database-notation-75d28eff-2509-4faf-8cd9-3eda5fb4327b

[10](DMBOK2, 125)

This page intentionally left blank.

Chapter 2 - Entities

Entities are used to describe how and what data is stored. As we model, an entity does not contain actual or sample data but contains data about the data. This is called metadata. This chapter will introduce and discuss the four type of entities: 1) categorical, 2) reference, 3) event/transaction, and 4) event/transaction detail. It also will discuss that we must strive to ensure that entities are clear, accurate, and complete.

Objectives

At the conclusion of this lesson module, students will be able to:

1. list and describe the four types of entities.
2. use the concept of an entity to describe a collection.

Four Types of Data in Entities

Data fall into four major categories:

1. categorical,
2. resource,
3. event/transaction, and
4. event/transaction detail.

Categorical Data

Categorical data is used to group other data elements, sometimes called indicators or flags. Examples include gender, language spoken, age group, and educational attainment level. Some categorical data is represented by alphabetic codes (like directions: N, NE, NW, S, SE, SW, E, W) but others are expressed as numbers (like spice level: 0, 1, 2, 3, 4, 5). When representing a category, like age, with a large range of values 0-110 it may be better to create categories representing a small groups or ranges (0-17, 18-24, 25-44, 45-64, 65+).

Below each of the four types of data will be tables of sample data and the symbols for the entity in the conceptual model format. The entity shape for the conceptual model, from Object Role Modeling 2 (ORM2), can be either an oval or a rounded rectangle. The rounded rectangle will be used in this text.

Gender

Table 1: Categorical - Gender Data

Code	Description
M	Male
F	Female

Code	Description
X	Other
NA	Not Answered

Figure 2: Categorical - Gender ORM2

Rating

Table 2: Categorical - Rating Data

Code	Description
0	No Opinion
1	Bad
2	Poor
3	Average
4	Good
5	Great

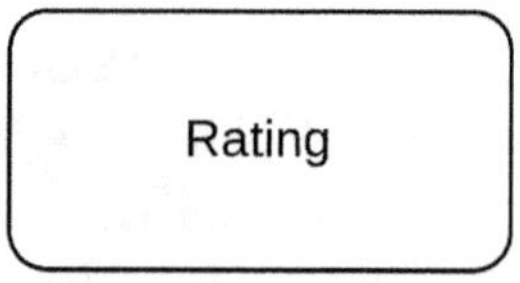

Figure 3: Categorical - Rating ORM2

Ledger Account Type

Table 3: Categorical - Ledger Account Type Data

accounttype_id	description
A	Asset

accounttype_id	description
L	Liability
C	Capital
I	Income
E	Expense

Figure 4: Categorical - Ledger Account Type ORM2

Categorical data that has only two possible values (Yes/No, Heads/Tails) is known as a binary variable or Boolean variable. A category with more than two possible values are known as multi-way or polytomous variables.

Categorical data is usually used in reporting summary data to calculate totals or counts.

Resource Data

Resource data represents data that is used to perform other operations. Resource data is slow changing. It represents the people, places, and things that event/transaction data and detail data affect. Example resource data includes: customers, vendors, locations, inventory items, and many more.

Company

Table 4: Resource - Company Data

company_id	description	taxid
1	FOO Consolidated	55-5559999
2	BAR Exploration	55-5559988
99	XYZ Sales	55-5559977

Figure 5: Resource - Company ORM2

General Ledger Accounts

Table 5: Resource - Ledger Accounts Data

account_id	description	accounttype_id
100	Cash	A
110	Accounts Receivable	A
190	Inventory	A
200	Accounts Payable	L
300	Shareholder Equity	C
390	Retained Earnings	C
400	Income	I
500	Supplies	E
510	Utilities	E
590	Cost of Goods Sold	E

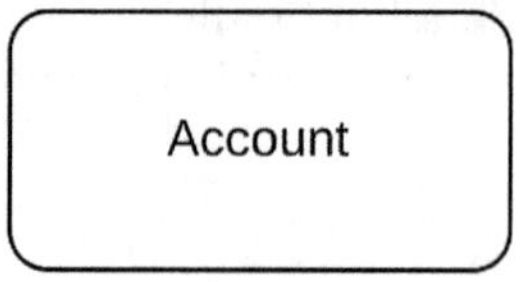

Figure 6: Resource - Ledger Accounts ORM2

Account Balance

Table 6: Resource - Account Balance Data

company_id	account_id	balance
1	100	500.0
1	190	500.0
1	300	-1000.0

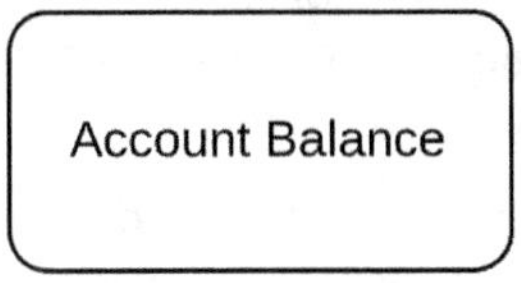

Figure 7: Resource - Account Balance ORM2

Event / Transaction Data

Event and transaction data is temporal in nature. Temporal means to relate to a sequence of time or to a specific time.[11] Event data is created and collected when something happens. Examples include: a sales order being created, a meeting happening, a purchase order being received, or the posting of a general ledger entry.

Ledger Transactions

Table 7: Event - Ledger Transaction Data

transaction_uuid	transactiondatetime	company_id	description
9e755caf-e250-11ef-8487-047c16fd53a0	2024-09-22 09:34:56	1	Initial Stock Purchase
afde0b67-e250-11ef-8487-047c16fd53a0	2024-09-22 11:33:30	1	Purchase Inventory

Figure 8: Event - Ledger Transaction ORM2

Event / Transaction Detail Data

Event and transaction detail data are all the small details usually associated with events. An example would be the detail lines, containing the specific debits and credits, on a general ledger entry. Another example of transaction data are

---

[11] https://www.merriam-webster.com/dictionary/temporal

the individual items and quantities of items on a single sales order. In a large database, there can be millions of these details that make up account balances, quantity on hand, and the totals of orders.

These detail transaction items are also used, in summary, to populate data warehouses and to answer a business's operational questions.

Details of Ledger Transactions

Table 8: Transaction - Ledger Transaction Data

transaction_uuid	account_id	amount
9e755caf-e250-11ef-8487-047c16fd53a0	100	1000.0
9e755caf-e250-11ef-8487-047c16fd53a0	300	-1000.0
afde0b67-e250-11ef-8487-047c16fd53a0	100	-500.0
afde0b67-e250-11ef-8487-047c16fd53a0	190	500.0

Figure 9: Transaction Detail - Ledger Transaction ORM2

Entities are Metadata

Entities are core metadata. They represent essential data about data they must strive to have:

- Clarity - The definition and existence of an entity in a data model should reflect and why it is included. Entities should have meaningful names that follow business rules.
- Accuracy - The definition needs to be precise and reviewed by subject-matter experts in the business.
- Completeness - All attributes need to be fully defined. The domain (range or list of values) of each attribute need to be defined.

Case - Neighborhood Bodega

Consider we are going to model the entities that describe the sales of a small neighborhood bodega.[12] The store creates a sales ticket in the ticket

---

[12]https://www.merriam-webster.com/dictionary/bodega

book for each customer order. An order may have one or more items on it. Each item on the shelf has a bar code, price, and cost (coded with letters). Items may belong to several different classifications: taxable/non-taxable, grocery/dairy/sundry/tobacco/alcohol, frozen/refrigerated/other.

Entities	Type
Customer	Resource Data
Ticket	Event Data
Item	Resource Data
Taxable	Categorical Data
Product Line	Categorical Data
Storage Needs	Categorical Data

Note: You may be tempted to make the bodega itself an entity. All the entities are part of the store, and we would not need to include it. If the problem stated that we had a chain of several bodegas and wanted to model the group of them, then the bodega/store would be an entity.

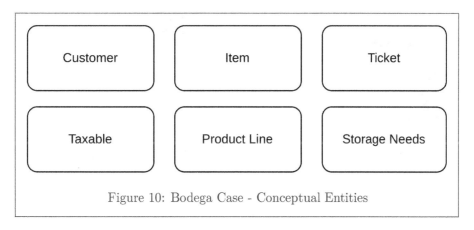

Figure 10: Bodega Case - Conceptual Entities

Additional entities may be needed to track the supplier/vendor of an item, when we last purchased an item, and current inventory. But these were not in the original problem.

Exercises

1. List and describe the entities in the following scenario (be sure to identify which of the four types each entity belongs to):

   A small dental office with multiple providers (dentists and hygienists). Patients make an appointment with a specific provider. An appointment consists of one or more service (filling, cleaning, extraction...).

2. List and describe the entities in the following scenario (be sure to identify which of the four types each entity belongs to):

There are many bowlers that compete in the bowling league in your area. A meet may be between two or more bowlers at an arranged time at one of five different bowling alleys. At the meet, each bowler plays one game and their score is recorded. The highest score wins the meet.

3. List and describe the entities in the following scenario (be sure to identify which of the four types each entity belongs to):

A trucking company operates a fleet of company owned trucks and employs several drivers. A driver and a truck are assigned to a load. A driver may be a local or long-distance driver. A load has an origin (starting point), a destination (ending point), and is billed to a customer.

Chapter 3 - Relationships Between Entities (CDM)

This chapter is all about relationships and drawing entities and simple relationships to create a Conceptual Data Model (CDM). The CDM will be drawn as a simplified Object Role Model 2. (ORM2) is type of **fact-oriented modeling**. This introduction of ORM2 modeling is brief and just discusses a very small part of this complicated communication technique.

Objectives

At the conclusion of this lesson module, students will be able to:

1. understand arity in relationships and be able to define binary, unary, and ternary relationships.
2. relate entities together through defining rules with cardinality.
3. describe entities as a subtype of another entity.
4. follow a defined approach to create a Conceptual Data Model of a real world data problem.

Arity of Relationships

Arity is a mathematical term that represents the count of values a function or operator takes.[13] In data modeling, arity refers to how many entities are part of a relationship. Most of the time data modelers will discover a situation can be described with three different types of relationships: 1) binary relationships, 2) unary relations, and 3) ternary relationships. There are in fact an unlimited number of possible combinations, but these three make up a vast majority of relationships. They will be discussed in the order that they are most often found.

Binary Relationship

A binary relationship exists between two entities. This relationship is drawn as a line with two boxes in the middle of it. These boxes may include cardinality (count) information or a text description of what the relationship is.

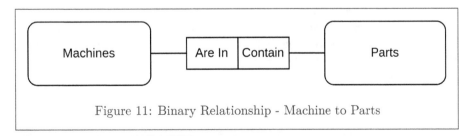

Figure 11: Binary Relationship - Machine to Parts

---

[13]https://www.webster-dictionary.org/definition/arity

17

In the example above, we can see the relationship between machines and parts that are used to make them up. A machine "contains" parts and parts "are in" one or more machines.

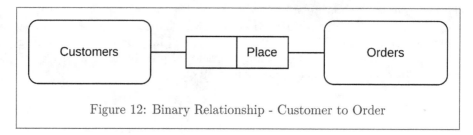

Figure 12: Binary Relationship - Customer to Order

In the second example, we can see that a customer "places" an order. The reverse relationship is not named, but the name can be inferred as "is placed by".

Unary (recursive) Relation

In a unary relationship, an entity can refer to itself. This is known as a **recursive** relationship.[14] These are significantly less common than the binary relation.

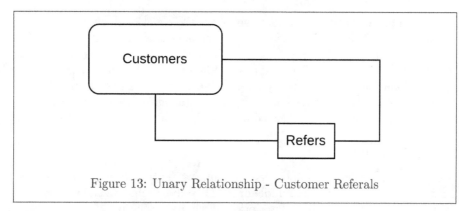

Figure 13: Unary Relationship - Customer Referals

In the diagram above, a customer may be referred by another customer. We may want to track if an existing customer told a new customer about our company. This data would help us to target advertising and reward the referring customer. Because this relationship is between two different customers, we would use a unary relation.

Ternary

A ternary relationship exists between three entities. Often this models something that depends on two entities or the detail information at the intersection of the

---

[14]https://www.merriam-webster.com/dictionary/recursive

two entities.

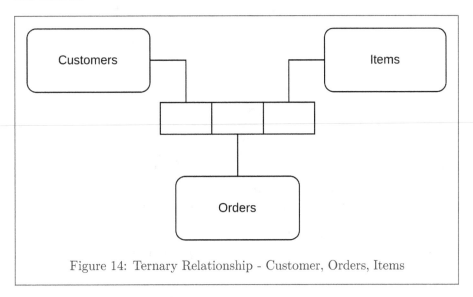

Figure 14: Ternary Relationship - Customer, Orders, Items

In the Customer - Order - Item relationship, a customer places an order for one or more items from our catalog. A customer does not have a direct relationship to an item. The relationship occurs through the customer purchasing it on an order.

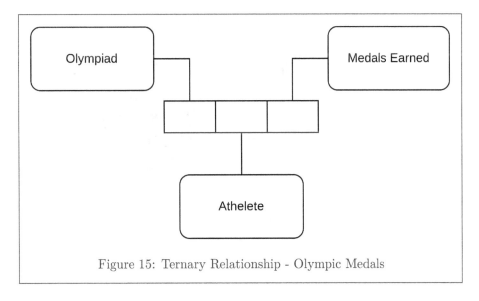

Figure 15: Ternary Relationship - Olympic Medals

Another ternary relationship example shows the relationship between an Olympiad (a set of games every four years) - an Athlete - and the Medals they have earned. If the relation was athlete to medals, then we would only be able to see lifetime medals from several different years. If the relation was Olympiad to medals, then we would only be able to see the medals earned during a year but not who they went to. By creating a ternary relationship we can see a medal and who and when it has been earned, an athlete and their medals for a game or lifetime, and many other combinations.

Cardinality of Relationships

Cardinality means the number of elements in a mathematical set.[15] In data modeling, cardinality refers to the number of entities on each side of a relationship. Let's go back to the binary relationship between a customer and an order.

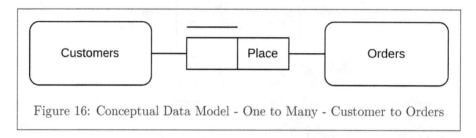

Figure 16: Conceptual Data Model - One to Many - Customer to Orders

The diagram above is slightly modified from the Customer - Order diagram in the Arity section. Notice that there is a bar above the left half of the binary relationship symbol. This bar means "At Most One". We can now read this diagram as "a customer may place any number of orders and an order may be placed by at most one customer". This little bar makes quite a difference.

Conceptual Data Model (CDM)

The diagrams you have seen so far in this chapter are Conceptual Data Models (CDMs) and show entities and the relationships between them.

In the following diagram, we model the relationship describing the ownership of a vehicle. The relationship is a binary relationship between the two entities: Person and Vehicle. A person "owns" a vehicle and a vehicle is owned by one person. A person may own zero, one, or many vehicles. A vehicle may have at most one owner (as denoted by the bar over half the relationship). Usually, a vehicle always has one owner, a new car is owned by the manufacturer or the dealer.

---

[15] https://www.merriam-webster.com/dictionary/cardinality

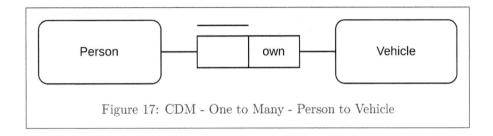

Figure 17: CDM - One to Many - Person to Vehicle

Let's look at another scenario: You are a stockbroker, and you sell stocks. An individual may have ownership rights to several portfolios or stocks (also thought of as accounts). A portfolio may have multiple owners. A portfolio holds shares in many different companies (stock) and a stock may be held in several portfolios. What does this look like?

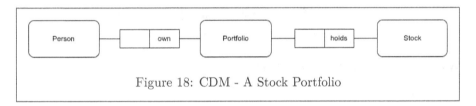

Figure 18: CDM - A Stock Portfolio

Yet another example, our website requires a registered user be associated with each blog post and a blog post must be associated to a single subject. It logically follows that a user can make several blog posts and that a subject has several blog posts.

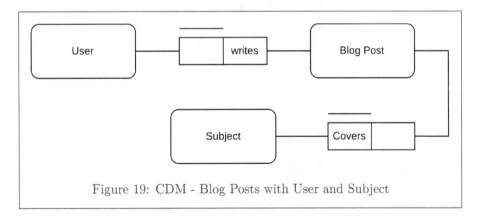

Figure 19: CDM - Blog Posts with User and Subject

Specialization and Generalization

Sometimes entities share major commonalities with other entities, we call this generalization. For example, a customer, vendor, or employee are all people and share much common information. We name this generalization an "is a" relationship. We can write this relationship as, a customer is a person and a vendor is a person and a employee is a person.

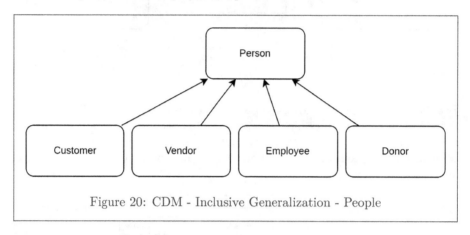

Figure 20: CDM - Inclusive Generalization - People

We may also work the other direction and divide an entity into specialized entities. A "has a" relationship. For example, your doctor may have one or more specialities.[16] They may specialize in areas, like: Family Medicine, Orthopedic Surgery, Oncology, or hundreds of others. We are working from the top down.

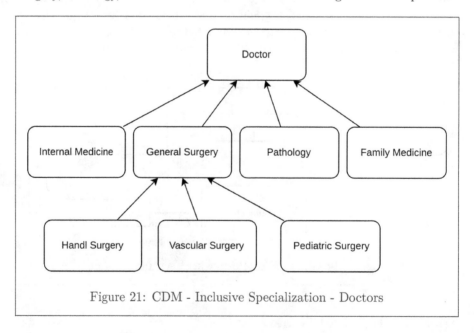

Figure 21: CDM - Inclusive Specialization - Doctors

This type of specialization and generalization in a data model is called by many

---

[16]https://careersinmedicine.aamc.org/explore-options/specialty-profiles

a 'Specialization Hierarchy' because the generalization and specialization can have many levels. In a CDM, an arrow is used to denote the "is a" relationship. Going against the flow of the arrow denotes a "has a" relationship.

The Specialization Hierarchy may be exclusive or inclusive. In an exclusive 'is a' relationship, an entity may only be one of the subtypes. An example of an exclusive relationship may be that a vehicle may be a motorcycle, automobile, or truck but not multiple types. The dotted line across the specialization/generalization arrows with the circled 'x' denotes this exclusive relationship. Inclusive relationships have no dotted line or other symbol shown.

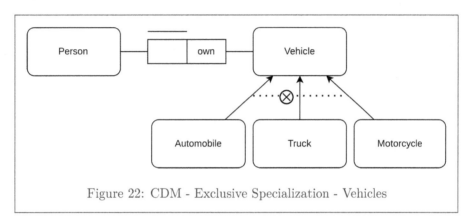

Figure 22: CDM - Exclusive Specialization - Vehicles

Case

Consider the neighbourhood bodega we looked at in the previous chapter.

The store creates a sales ticket in the ticket book for each customer order. An order may have one or more items on the order. Each item on the shelf has a bar code, price, and cost (coded with letters). Items belong to several different classifications: taxable/non-taxable, grocery/dairy/sundry/tobacco/alcohol, frozen/refrigerated/other.

Solution One - CDM

We identified the following entities and can identify the relationships. We see that most of the relationships are binary except for customer + item + ticket that is a ternary relationship.

Entities	Type	Relationship
Customer	Resource Data	Many tickets.
Ticket	Event Data	One customer, many items.

Entities	Type	Relationship
Item	Resource Data	Many tickets, one taxable, one product line, one storage needs.
Taxable	Categorical Data	Many items.
Product Line	Categorical Data	Many items.
Storage Needs	Categorical Data	Many items.

A conceptual data model (CDM) would look something like:

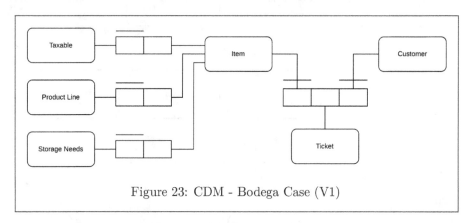

Figure 23: CDM - Bodega Case (V1)

Solution Two - CDM

We can also think of the same problem a different way. What if we add an entity that represents the detail information on a ticket, the 'Ticket Item Detail'. With this additional entity all the relationships become binary.

Entities	Type	Relationship
Customer	Resource Data	Many tickets.
Ticket	Event Data	One customer, many item details.
Ticket Item Detail	Event Detail Data	One ticket, one item.
Item	Resource Data	Many item details, one taxable, one product line, one storage needs.
Taxable	Categorical Data	Many items.
Product Line	Categorical Data	Many items.

Entities	Type	Relationship
Storage Needs	Categorical Data	Many items.

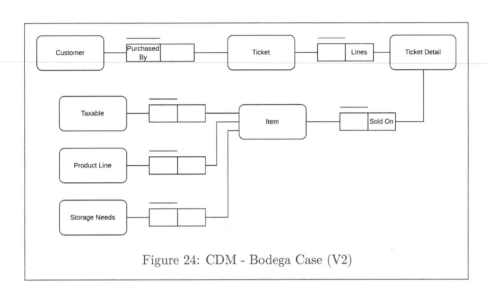

Figure 24: CDM - Bodega Case (V2)

Exercises

1. Draw a CDM for the following scenario:

   A small dental office with multiple providers (dentists and hygienists). Patients make an appointment with a specific provider. An appointment consists of one or more service (filling, cleaning, extraction...).

2. Draw a CDM for the following scenario:

   There are many bowlers that compete in the bowling league in your area. A meet may be between two or more bowlers at an arranged time at one of five different bowling alleys. At the meet, each bowler plays one game and their score is recorded. The highest score wins the meet.

3. Draw a CDM for the following scenario:

   A trucking company operates a fleet of company owned trucks and employs several drivers. A driver and a truck are assigned to a load. A driver may be a local or long-distance driver. A load has an origin (starting point), a destination (ending point), and is billed to a customer.

This page intentionally left blank.

Chapter 4 - Attributes

In the previous chapters, we have discussed entities and relationships between them. This chapter will discuss the properties of entities also known as attributes.

Objectives

At the conclusion of this lesson module, students will be able to:

1. identify the difference between a natural and synthetic attribute.
2. list and identify elements/attributes of an entity.
3. find the elements that are basic and critical to describe a collection of data.
4. draw an entity in the IE (crow's foot) ERD style with attributes and domains.

Attributes

Attributes are the properties of an entity. They are the actual data values that make each instance of an entity different. The owner entity data from our veterinarian's office sample data looks like:

Table 12: Owner Entity Sample Data

owner_id	last_name	first_name	phone	email
1	Smithson	Amy	1-555-555-3467	asmit89@notreal.com
2	Ralston	Howard	1-555-555-6712	howie88@notreal.com
3	Greene	Susan	1-555-555-5543	catwoman@notreal.com
4	Luton	Lex	1-555-555-9988	lexlex@notreal.com
5	Clark	John	1-555-555-8111	johnnyc@notreal.com

There are five attributes, columns, that make up the owner entity: owner_id, last_name, first_name, phone, and email. Each row in the table represents a different owner.

Table 13: Owner Entity Attributes

Attribute	Domain	Description
owner_id	integer	Assigned customer number. The next available number will be assigned a new customer.
last_name	string	A string of letters with the customer's last name.
first_name	string	A string of letters with the customer's first name.
phone	string	A string of letters with the customer's phone number.
email	string	A string of letters with the customer's fully qualified email address.

An attribute is given a name and the data stored in an attribute should be atomic. Atomic, in relation to data modeling, means a single value. An attribute should also have a domain that represents the range of values that it should contain.

Attribute Origin

Attributes either originate directly from the entity (natural) or are created/generated/assigned by the system or application (synthetic).

Natural Attributes

A natural attribute describes or contains an inherent property of the entity itself. An entity, if it has awareness, knows these things about itself. These attributes may change over an entity's life cycle.

Common natural attributes in a database include:

- name / description,
- address / location,
- weight / size,
- cost / price,
- birth / creation date,
- and countless others.

Synthetic Attributes

A synthetic attribute is one that has meaning to the system or database and was created for a special reason. They are typically used to uniquely identify an entity. Synthetic attributes usually fall into three broad categories: 1) sequentially assigned identifiers, 2) random sequences, or 3) abbreviations.

In the example above, we assigned each owner a unique synthetic and sequential ID number (identifier). It is common for an entity to be given a number to uniquely identify it for the life of the system. At your university or school, you were assigned a student number and no student will ever have that same number at your school. Sometimes, there sequentially assigned identifiers may contain alphabetic characters, like the license plate number on your car.

For transactional data that may be created by multiple applications in different locations, it becomes difficult to have a single issuer of the next sequential number to use as an identifier. One could use a sufficiently large random number as an identifier. One such numbering scheme is the 128 bit Universally Unique Identifier (UUID).[17]

The third type of synthetic attributes are abbreviations or acronyms used to shorten names or descriptions into small unique identifiers that are easily

---

[17]https://en.wikipedia.org/wiki/Universally_unique_identifier

remembered. Examples include: M for Male, F for Female, NASA for National Aeronautics and Space Administration, or JMR for James M. Reneau Ph.D.

Naming Attributes and Entities

There is no standard for how to name entities and attributes, but there are four very common ways to write identifiers in SQL. They are:

- PascalCase - The first letter of each word is capitalized.[18]
- camelCase - The first letter of the second and subsequent word is capitalized.
- snake_case - No letters are capitalized, but underscores are placed between words.
- lowercase - All letters are lower case and words have no separator.

Recommendations

1. Entity names and attribute names should begin with a letter and contain only letters, numbers, and underscores.
2. One style should be adopted and used throughout a single database or enterprise.
3. Abbreviations need to be used consistently.
4. Entity names should be singular or plural, such as: customer vs. customers or city vs. cities.

Inconsistency will slow development, make maintenance more expensive, and may contribute to bugs and issues with your applications.

Domain of an Attribute

Attributes also have a type or **domain**. The domain is the valid range of values to be stored in that attribute of that entity. All modern databases minimally implement the storage of fixed precision numbers, floating point numbers, strings, Boolean values, datetimes, and binary objects but the specifics of ranges and features may vary.

- Fixed precision decimal number (INTEGER or DECIMAL)

  - An integer (whole number) is usually stored as a 16 bit (-32,768 through 32,767), 32 bit (-2,147,483,648 through 2,147,483,647), or 64 bit (-9,223,372,036,854,775,808 through 9,223,372,036,854,775,807) signed number.

  - A fixed precision decimal number will store a specified number of digits before and after the decimal point. These are usually used for exact measurements or for currencies.

- Floating point number (FLOAT)

---

[18]https://builtin.com/articles/pascal-case-vs-camel-case

- A floating point number is stored in scientific notation with a significand and exponent.[19] This allows for values with large magnitudes but with limited precision. Remember numbers stored in this type are approximations and may not be exact.

- String (STRING)

  - A string is a sequence of letters, numbers, and other symbols.[20] Names, addresses, and many identifiers are stored as string values. Strings may be variable length with a maximum storage length or a fixed length.

- Boolean value (BOOL)

  - The Boolean type was named for mathematician George Boole, who studied the algebra of true and false values.[21] The Boolean attribute will store one of two values: 1) true, or 2) false.[22] In some databases, this type of value may be stored in an integer field as 0 for false and `not` 0 (1, -1, ...) as true.

- Date and time (DATETIME)

  - A single value including a date and time together expressed in ISO format (YYYY-MM-DD HH:MM:SS.SSS).[23] Some databases have specific data types to store dates and times as separate attributes, but for simplicity in this text we will only be using `DATETIME`.

- Binary objects (BLOB)

  - Binary object attributes are used to store sound, video, encrypted strings, or other binary data.[24]

Attributes may be allowed to be empty or required. We call the empty value NULL. In fact, NULL is not a value it represents nothingness.

Entity Relationship Diagram - Entity Shape

Now that we have defined attributes with their domains we are ready to start moving into the Logical Data Model (LDM). There are several different techniques for drawing an LDM but the style we will be using is known as an IE ERD, a Crows Foot ERD, or simply an ERD.

The shape for an entity, in an ERD, is a rectangle divided into sections with the top section containing the entity name and the bottom sections containing the

---

[19] https://en.wikipedia.org/wiki/Significand
[20] https://en.wikipedia.org/wiki/String_(computer_science)
[21] https://www.britannica.com/biography/George-Boole
[22] https://www.geeksforgeeks.org/boolean-data-type/
[23] https://en.wikipedia.org/wiki/ISO_8601
[24] https://dev.mysql.com/doc/refman/8.4/en/blob.html

attributes. Types and other notations may be included to add more detail to the model.

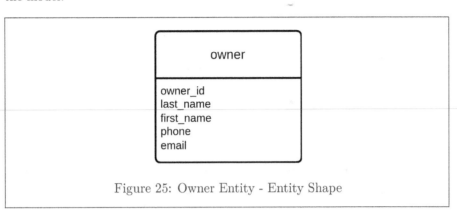

Figure 25: Owner Entity - Entity Shape

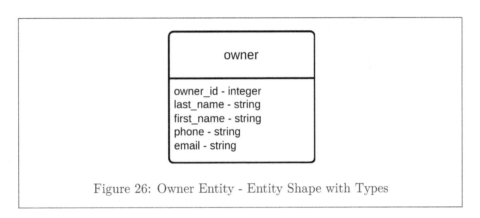

Figure 26: Owner Entity - Entity Shape with Types

Case One - Neighborhood Bodega

Consider the neighborhood bodega we looked at in the previous two chapters.

To recap: The store creates a sales ticket in the ticket book for each customer order. An order may have one or more items on the order. Each item on the shelf has a bar code, price, and cost (coded with letters). Items belong to several different classifications: taxable/non-taxable, grocery/dairy/sundry/tobacco/alcohol, frozen/refrigerated/other.

We identified the following entities and now need to identify attributes for each of them. If we were working with a real client, we would collect artifacts and interview the client to see what data they collect and want to collect on the entities. In this situation, we will use our general business knowledge to list common attributes for this example.

Entities	Type
Customer	Resource Data
Ticket	Event Data
Ticket Item Detail	Event Detail Data
Item	Resource Data
Taxable	Categorical Data
Product Line	Categorical Data
Storage Needs	Categorical Data

Customer

Attribute	Domain	Description
name	string	what name we have (first, first/last, nickname, company. . .)
address	string	delivery address
city	string	
state	string	
post_code	string	
phone_number	string	customer's phone number (just digits - no dashes)
email	string	

Ticket

Attribute	Domain	Description
ticket_number	integer	pre-printed unique number on ticket book
order_datetime	datetime	
sales_clerk_initials	string	
customer_phone_number	string	optional if not delivery order
delivery_address	string	empty if not delivery order
non_tax_total	decimal	total of non-taxable items
taxable_total	decimal	total of taxable items
tax	decimal	sales tax calculated on taxable_total
total	decimal	sum of non_tax_total, taxable_total, and tax
payment_method	string	C-Cash, CK-Check, D-Debit, CR-Credit Card, EBT-EBT Card
payment_auth	string	authorization number or check number

Ticket Item Detail

Attribute	Domain	Description
ticket_number	integer	
item_description	string	
price	decimal	
taxable_code	string	
quantity	decimal	most items we sell whole products but for others we sell by pound
total	decimal	price times quantity

Item

Attribute	Domain	Description
upc	string	UPC Barcode - Most items have
description	string	item description
price	decimal	current selling price
cost	decimal	average cost of item in inventory
taxable_code	string	default taxable status on ticket
line_code	string	product line
storage_code	string	storage requirements code

Taxable

Attribute	Domain	Description
taxable_code	string	
tax_district	string	name of taxing district or rate
rate	decimal	percentage tax rate

Product Line

Attribute	Domain	Description
line_code	string	
description	string	

Storage Needs

Attribute	Domain	Description
storage_code	string	
description	string	
min_temp	decimal	minimum storage temperature in F

Attribute	Domain	Description
max_temp	decimal	maximum storage temperature in F

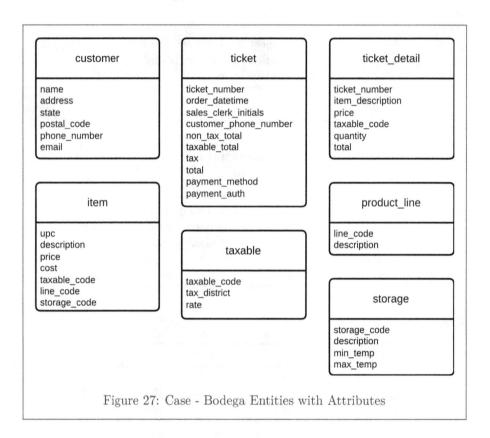

Figure 27: Case - Bodega Entities with Attributes

Case Two - Sensor Readings

You have a client with sensors scattered around their facility. Each sensor has a unique identifier and measures temperature, pressure, or rotation. It will return a numeric observation value, and the units associated to that value. The client has given us a sample spreadsheet with representative data. Each row represents a moment in the past (temporal data) for a specific sensor.

Table 22: Sensor Reading Data

SensorID	SensorType	ReadingDateTime	Reading	Units
A23	TEMP	2024-09-21 10:00	23	C
A23	TEMP	2024-09-21 11:00	23.5	C
X33	PRES	2024-09-21 00:00	1.03	ATM

SensorID	SensorType	ReadingDateTime	Reading	Units
X33	PRES	2024-09-21 12:01	1.02	ATM
F87	ROT	2024-09-21 12:01	55	DEG

The client has also given us definitions of each of the columns in the spreadsheet. This includes the domain (range/type) of each column and a brief description.

Table 23: Sensor Reading Attributes

Attribute	Domain	Description
SensorID	string	A unique alphanumeric code assigned to each sensor.
SensorType	string	A string representing type of sensor. Valid values are TEMP, PRES, and ROT,
ReadingDateTime	datetime	Date and time of the reading.
Reading	decimal	Decimal value read by sensor.
Units	string	String representing the unit associated with the read value.

If we look at the data and understand it, we will see the following conceptual relationship between sensors, their types, and the units of a reading. A possible conceptual data model (CDM) might look like:

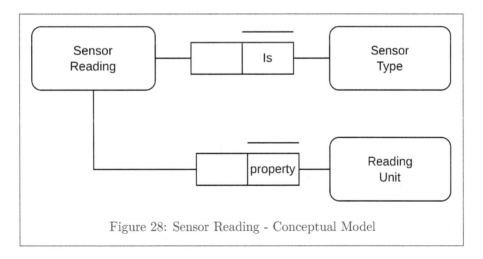

Figure 28: Sensor Reading - Conceptual Model

CDM's do not typically include attributes, so we need to use the new ERD Entity shape to include the attributes, and optionally their types.

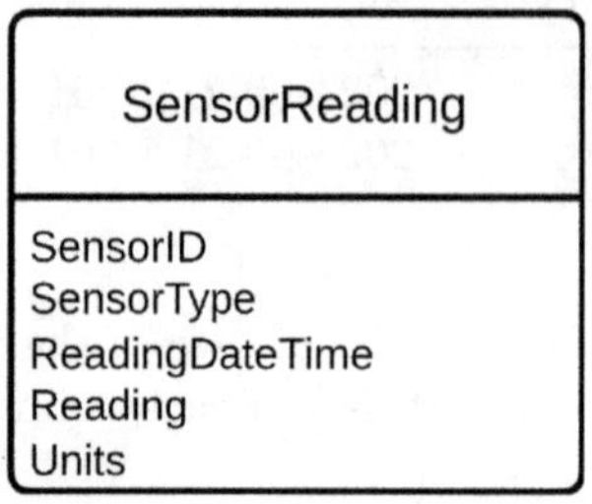

Figure 29: Sensor Reading - Entity Shape

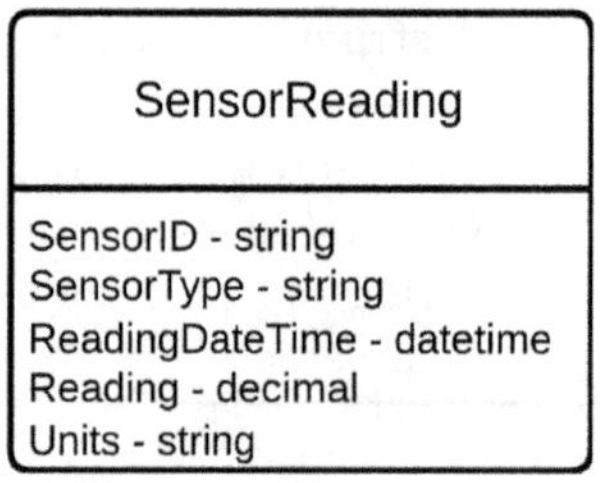

Figure 30: Sensor Reading - Entity Shape with Types

Exercises

1. Define the terms 'natural attribute' and 'synthetic attribute' in your own words. Be sure to list a few attributes of each type in your discussion.
2. Most databases implement the following generic types of attributes: integers, fixed precision numbers, floating point numbers, strings, Boolean values, datetimes, and binary objects. Define each in your own words and include a few attributes that would belong to these types.
3. List several attributes of a book. Identify their types and draw the ERD Entity shape for your book entity.
4. List several attributes of an item for sale in a store. Identify their types and draw the ERD Entity shape for your dog entity.

Chapter 5 - Keys

In the previous chapter, we have introduced the ERD Entity shape and have added attributes to that modeling shape. To be implemented in a database, and to be useful, we will need to identify or add one or more keys. A key is an attribute or combination of attributes that will be used to identify a specific row in a table.

Objectives

At the conclusion of this lesson module, students will be able to:

1. define a key.
2. list and discuss the five attributes of a key.
3. create a list of candidate keys for an entity.
4. choose a primary key from the list of candidate keys.
5. create and use a surrogate key.

What is a Key?

A key is an attribute or several attributes when taken together that uniquely identifies a row. Keys are used to create indexes for fast lookup, to retrieve a specific row, and to create relationships between entities. An entity may have multiple keys defined. A key needs to be: unique, non-volatile, minimal, not null, and secure.

Unique

To be effectively used to retrieve a single instance of an entity (row), duplicate values of the key may not exist. A key must uniquely identify one and only one row. Examples of unique attributes may include: order number, serial number, or other sequentially assigned identifiers. The attributes of name, address, birthday, and phone may seem unique, but two people could live at the same address, share an email address, or even have the same name.

Non-volatile

The attribute or attributes chosen to used as a key should be ones that do not change. An example would be a customer that wants to change their email address from one provided by their employer to a personal one. Even a person's or company's name may change.

Minimal

A key should be as small as possible to uniquely identify an instance of an entity. This is especially true for composite keys. Combine the least number of attributes possible to uniquely identify a row.

Not NULL

Attributes that may be NULL may not be used as keys or parts of keys.

Secure

Lastly, the attribute or group of attributes that we define as a key need to be secure. By secure, we do not mean that a key needs to be kept hidden or secret. A key should not be a value or contain a value that may be private or confidential. Using a Government Issued Identifier (Social Security Number, Passport Number, Driver's License Number...) or other Personally Identifiable Information (PII) is a bad practice even though it meets the other criteria for a good key.

Simple Key or Composite Key

In many situations, we will have a single attribute or several individual attributes, joined together, that would meet the criteria for a good key.

A single attribute used as a key is called a **Simple Key**. Examples of simple keys may include: an identifying abbreviation, UPC, email, phone, customer number, member code, and many more. There are probably several single attributes on an entity that would satisfy the criteria of a good simple key.

Composite/Compound Key

Keys may also be made by concatenating multiple attributes together into a single key.[25] This is type of key is called a **Composite Key**. Composite keys, where several attributes are concatenated together, are very commonlt used in relational databases.

There is a special type of composite key that is made up of only foreign keys, known as a **Compound Key**. Foreign keys will be covered and examples of compound keys will be shown in the *Logical Data Model (LDM)* chapter.

For example, we have an entity that contains the inventory we have in our stores. The attributes would be store number, item number, and the quantity on hand in each store. It would look like this:

Table 24: Store Inventory Data

store_number	item_number	quantity_on_hand
12	345	4
12	1010	3
12	8765	8
34	345	3

---

[25]https://www.merriam-webster.com/dictionary/concatenate

store_number	item_number	quantity_on_hand
34	1010	5
56	1010	4
56	8765	12
56	9090	2

Table 25: Store Inventory Attributes

Attribute	Domain	Description
store_number	integer	Unique identifier for store.
item_number	integer	Unique identifier for item
quantity_on_hand	integer	Quantity in a store for a specific item.

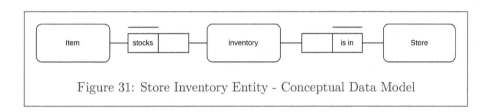

Figure 31: Store Inventory Entity - Conceptual Data Model

We can see that store_number does not uniquely identify a single row, nor does item_number. If we concatenate them together, then we can uniquely identify a single row with a composite key. We could have concatenated all three columns together but that then would violate the principles that a key should be minimal (as small as possible) and non-volatile (it would change every time the quantity on hand changed)

Candidate and Primary Keys

An entity may have several different keys that meet the criteria of a good key. We call these **candidate keys**. These candidate keys will be used for indexing and retrieval. For example, a customer file may have a customer number and an email address, with the business rule that each email address can only be used by one customer. Both would be candidate keys and both would be used by different applications and at different times.

Primary Key

Once we have identified our candidate key or keys, it is time to select one of them to be used throughout the database as the unique identifier for each row of this entity. This selected key is called the **Primary Key**.

39

Usually the primary key will be the simplest of the candidate keys. An entity must have only one primary key.

Natural Key or Surrogate Key

The candidate keys we find, in an attribute, can be thought of as **Natural Keys**. They occur naturally in the data. An entity usually knows this fact about itself and would recognize it as an identifier.

Surrogate Key

Database designers will sometimes assign an arbitrary number or code as the key. This assigned, synthetic attribute, that will be used as a key, is called a **Surrogate Key**. If the surrogate key is a single attribute, which it usually is, it is a special type of simple key.

A surrogate key may be created; 1) when there is not a good natural key (either simple or compound), 2) as an additional key, or 3) to replace a complex composite key to simplify the database structure.

The surrogate key is often a sequentially assigned number, random code, or UUID. It has no real meaning in association to the row of the entity.

Using a surrogate key instead of a composite key will often make the design of the database significantly more efficient. Surrogate keys are also very helpful when combining records from multiple sources where there could be duplications.

There is no strict rule for when to use a surrogate key vs. a natural key as the primary key. If it makes the database structure simpler and easier to model, then it probably is a good idea to use one.

Adding the Primary Key to the LDM

There are several different ways to denote the primary key currently in use by data modelers. Some will add the letters "PK" or an asterisk "*" before or after the attribute/attributes that make up the primary key. In this introduction, the attribute/attributes that are used as the primary key will be in a bold font and usually shown as first attributes.

More examples of Entities with Attributes and Keys

These examples come from the previous chapter on entities where the Conceptual Data Model shape was shown. Here we take the conceptual diagram and draw it with attributes and with the primary key identified.

Categorical Data

Gender

Table 26: Categorical - Gender Data

Code	Description
M	Male
F	Female
X	Other
NA	Not Answered

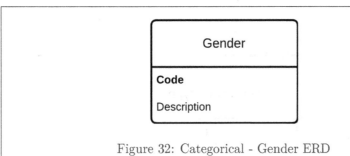

Figure 32: Categorical - Gender ERD

Rating

Table 27: Categorical - Rating Data

Code	Description
0	No Opinion
1	Bad
2	Poor
3	Average
4	Good
5	Great

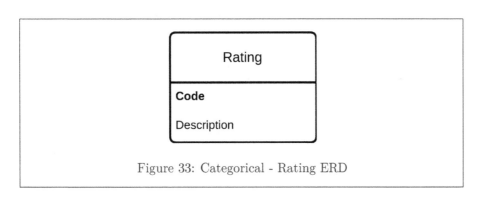

Figure 33: Categorical - Rating ERD

Ledger Account Type

Table 28: Categorical - Ledger Account Type Data

accounttype_id	description
A	Asset
L	Liability
C	Capital
I	Income
E	Expense

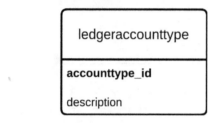

Figure 34: Categorical - Ledger Account Type ERD

Resource Data

Company

Table 29: Resource - Company Data

company_id	description	taxid
1	FOO Consolidated	55-5559999
2	BAR Exploration	55-5559988
99	XYZ Sales	55-5559977

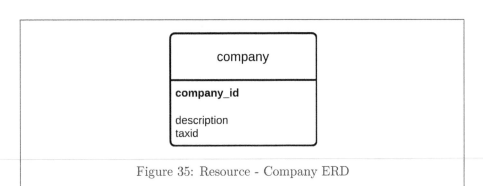

Figure 35: Resource - Company ERD

General Ledger Accounts

Table 30: Resource - Ledger Accounts Data

account_id	description	accounttype_id
100	Cash	A
110	Accounts Receivable	A
190	Inventory	A
200	Accounts Payable	L
300	Shareholder Equity	C
390	Retained Earnings	C
400	Income	I
500	Supplies	E
510	Utilities	E
590	Cost of Goods Sold	E

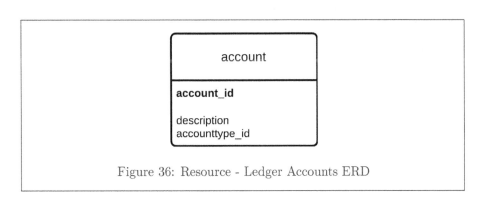

Figure 36: Resource - Ledger Accounts ERD

Account Balance

Table 31: Resource - Account Balance Data

company_id	account_id	balance
1	100	500.0
1	190	500.0
1	300	-1000.0

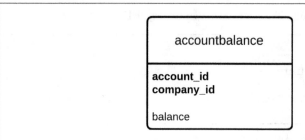

Figure 37: Resource - Account Balance ERD

Event Data

Ledger Transactions

The 'ledgertransaction' table uses a special type of value known as a Universally Unique Identifier (UUID). It is an identifier that should be unique across the globe.

transaction_uuid	transactiondatetime	company_id	description
9e755caf-e250-11ef-8487-047c16fd53a0	2024-09-22 09:34:56	1	Initial Stock Purchase
afde0b67-e250-11ef-8487-047c16fd53a0	2024-09-22 11:33:30	1	Purchase Inventory

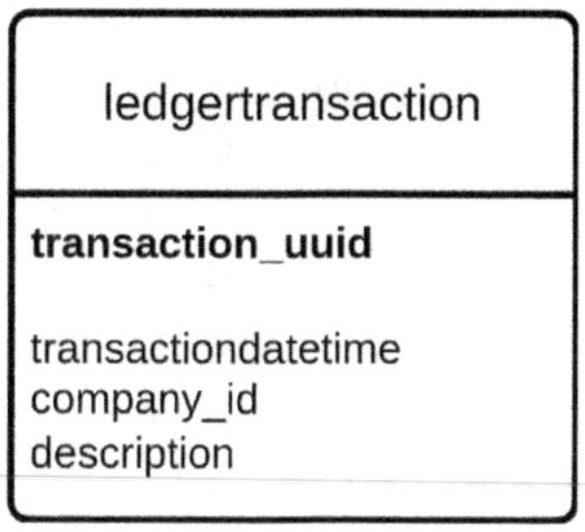

Figure 38: :Event - Ledger Transaction ERD

Detail Transaction Data

Details of Ledger Transactions

Table 33: Transaction - Ledger Transaction Data

transaction_uuid	account_id	amount
9e755caf-e250-11ef-8487-047c16fd53a0	100	1000.0
9e755caf-e250-11ef-8487-047c16fd53a0	300	-1000.0
afde0b67-e250-11ef-8487-047c16fd53a0	100	-500.0
afde0b67-e250-11ef-8487-047c16fd53a0	190	500.0

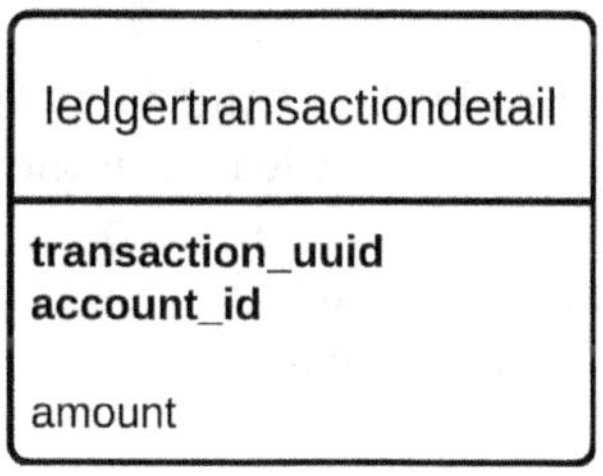

Figure 39: Transaction - Ledger Transaction ERD

Case One - Neighborhood Bodega

Consider the neighborhood bodega we looked at in the previous chapters.

We have identified entities and many attributes, but we need to identify keys for each attribute. For some this will be trivial but for others we will need to look at what the client wants from the data. Let us go through each entity, identify candidate keys and pick the best or use a surrogate key.

Customer

The customer entity is used to look up the delivery address and to potentially mail flyers or send emails about specials. Candidate keys include: 1) customer name concatenated with address (there could be two people with the same name or two different customers at the same address), 2) phone number, 3) email address, or 4) we could add a customer number as a surrogate key.

Customers usually phone in delivery orders with a call or text, so a phone number would make a good key. We don't have to worry about security, and people don't change their phone numbers often.

Ticket

This one is trivial. We possibly could concatenate multiple fields together but what if a customer came in twice in a day, paid cash, and bought the same candy-bar from the same sales clerk? I would suggest using the ticket_number pre-printed on the ticket book page as a simple primary key.

Item

The item has a couple of potential candidate keys: 1) the description could be one if they were unique or 2) UPC barcode number if every item has one. In this case, I would suggest adding an item_code attribute where we could assign a unique alphabetic identifier to each item, like (SKIMHALF, SKIMGAL, COKE12, COKE20...). We can use the description or the UPC code to look up an item's code.

Ticket Detail

The ticket_detail entity originally stored the item_description but should store the item_code. If the description is needed, then the item_code attribute could be used to get it. There are really two good choices: 1) create a composite key by concatenating ticket_number and item_code, or 2) add a surrogate key and assign each row on a ticket a unique number. I would recommend the first.

Taxable

The taxing district name or code would make a good candidate keys, but the code seems tailor-made as a good primary key.

Product Line

The product line description or code would make a good candidate keys. The code would be the better primary key.

Storage Needs

Possible candidate keys could be; 1) the storage_code, 2) the description, or 3) built by concatenating the temperatures together. The storage_code would be the better of the three.

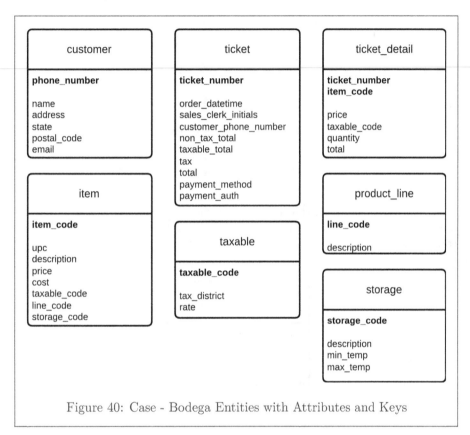

Figure 40: Case - Bodega Entities with Attributes and Keys

Case Two - Sensor Readings

Let us take the case from the previous chapter on Attributes and see what we can use for a key.

Remember: we have a client with sensors scattered around their facility. We have a sample spreadsheet with representative data. Each row represents a sensor's reading.

Table 34: Sensor Reading Data

SensorID	SensorType	ReadingDateTime	Reading	Units
A23	TEMP	2024-09-21 10:00	23	C

SensorID	SensorType	ReadingDateTime	Reading	Units
A23	TEMP	2024-09-21 11:00	23.5	C
X33	PRES	2024-09-21 00:00	1.03	ATM
X33	PRES	2024-09-21 12:01	1.02	ATM
F87	ROT	2024-09-21 12:01	55	DEG

Solution One - Composite Key

As we look at the data, we can see that there is not a single attribute that uniquely identifies a row. Which attributes can we concatenate together to create a good composite primary key? Always remembering that a key should be unique, non-volatile, minimal, not null, and secure.

There do not appear to be any sensitive data in the columns, so we are secure. There are no null values, so we are not null. Also, once a reading is made it does not change, so each row is non-volatile. We just need unique and minimal.

We could concatenate all the columns together and call it a day. It would be unique, but that would not be a minimal solution. The best solution for a composite key would be to take the SeasorID and ReadingDateTime together.

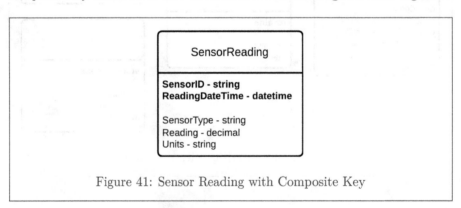

Figure 41: Sensor Reading with Composite Key

Solution Two - A Surrogate Key

A second possible solution would be to assign each reading, as we save it to the database a unique number (shown) or a UUID.

Table 35: Sensor Reading Data with Surrogate Key

ReadingNumber	SensorID	SensorType	ReadingDateTime	Reading	Units
1	A23	TEMP	2024-09-21 10:00	23	C
2	A23	TEMP	2024-09-21 11:00	23.5	C
3	X33	PRES	2024-09-21 00:00	1.03	ATM

ReadingNumber	SensorID	SensorType	ReadingDateTime	Reading	Units
4	X33	PRES	2024-09-21 12:01	1.02	ATM
5	F87	ROT	2024-09-21 12:01	55	DEG

We could now use the new attribute (ReadingNumber) as a primary key. It meets all the requirements of a good key.

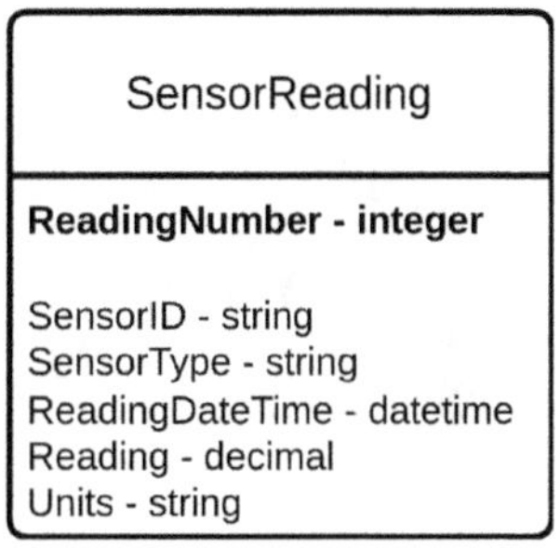

SensorReading

ReadingNumber - integer

SensorID - string
SensorType - string
ReadingDateTime - datetime
Reading - decimal
Units - string

Figure 42: Sensor Reading with Surrogate Key

Exercises

1. List the five attributes of a good key and define each in your own words.
2. In the attributes chapter, you listed several attributes of a book. Identify the candidate keys and pick the best one as your primary key. Write a brief discussion of your choices.
3. Define the following terms in your own words, giving examples:
   - Simple Key
   - Composite Key
   - Compound Key
   - Surrogate Key
   - Candidate Keys
   - Primary Key
4. In the attributes chapter, you listed several attributes of an item for sale in a store. Identify the candidate keys and pick the best one as your primary key. Write a brief discussion of your choices.

This page intentionally left blank.

Chapter 6 - Logical Data Model (LDM)

In the previous couple of chapters, we have learned to draw an Entity shape with all attributes and primary key designated. Now that we can draw them, we need to add the relationships between them to create a Logical Data Model (LDM).

Objectives

At the conclusion of this lesson module, students will be able to:

1. identity, create, and use a foreign key to implement a relationship between entities.
2. take a Conceptual Data Model (CDM) into Logical Data Model (LDM)
3. draw a crows-foot Entity Relation Diagram (ERD).

There are several different methods for drawing logical and physical data models. Three commonly used techniques are the IDEF1X, the Information Engineering (IE) model, and the Chen Notation.[26] [27] [28] This text will use a common variant of the IE model, also sometimes called the 'crows-foot' notation because of the line endings.

The LDM

In an IE style Logical Data Model, we draw a line with special end symbols to define the cardinality of a relationship. Lines may end with one of four symbols:

Line End Symbol	Description
	One and only one.
	Zero or one.
	One or more.

[26] https://www.idef.com/idef1x-data-modeling-method/

[27] Finkelstein, C. (1989) An Introduction to Information Engineering. Addison-Wesley.

[28] Chen, P. (1977) The Entity-Relationship Model: Toward a Unified View of Data. Center for Information Systems Research. Massachusetts Institute of Technology. CISR No. 30, WP 913-77. Retrieved from https://dspace.mit.edu/bitstream/handle/1721.1/47432/entityrelationshx00chen.pdf

Line End Symbol	Description
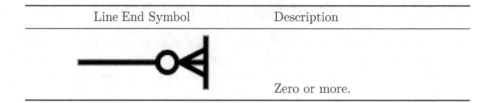	
	Zero or more.

One of these arrow ends are placed on each end of a relationship. An optional description of the relationship may also be added to the relationship for clarity.

For example, let us look at the relationship between an animal and their species. An animal must be one and only one species and a species may have several animals. Our partially complete LDM may look like:

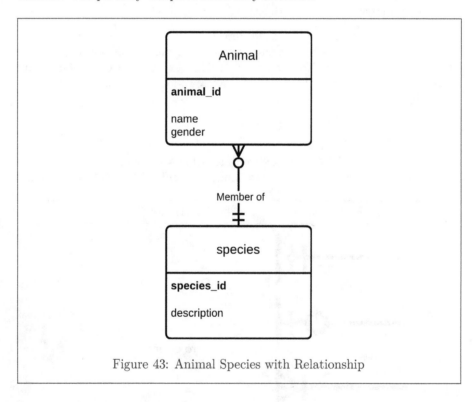

Figure 43: Animal Species with Relationship

This diagram can be read as an animal is one and only one species and a species may have zero or more animals.

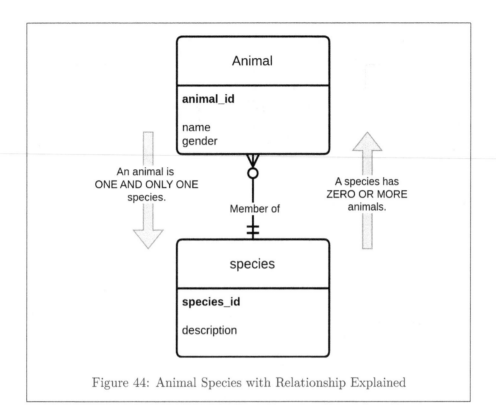

Figure 44: Animal Species with Relationship Explained

Another example may be for an auto parts store. A customer has zero or more orders, an order must have a customer and one or more parts on it, and a part may be on zero or more orders.

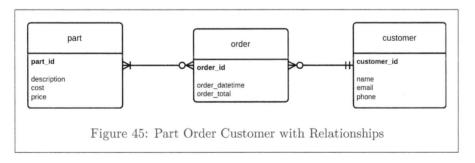

Figure 45: Part Order Customer with Relationships

Here is the same diagram with extra arrows explaining the relationships.

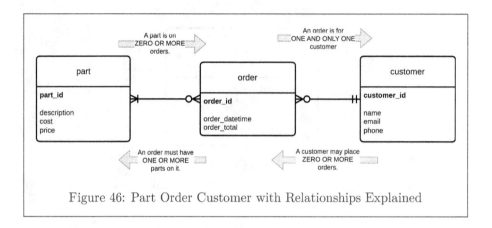

Figure 46: Part Order Customer with Relationships Explained

Foreign Key

To implement a one-to-one or one-to-many relationship, we will create an attribute or attributes that will contain the primary key of the "one" table on the "many" table. This is called a **foreign key** and on our ERDs it will be marked with an '(FK)' . Later we will use it in our database to connect the tables together and to maintain integrity of our relationships. You can think of it as a way to move from one table to another.

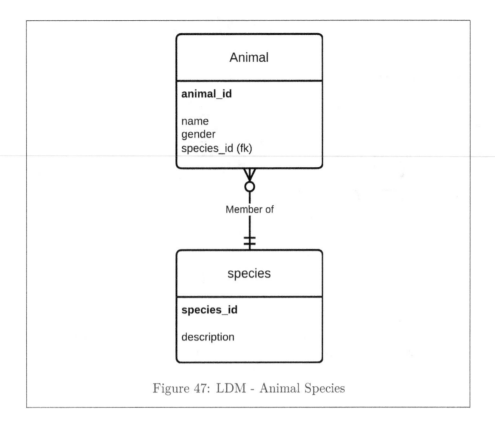

Figure 47: LDM - Animal Species

Remove Many-to-Many Relationships

There is a problem with the part/order/customer diagram, above. How and where do we store the quantity purchased of each item for each order? If we store it on the order table, then all parts must have the same order quantity. Or if we store it on the parts table then all orders must have the same quantity of a part. In a CDM, this still works, but in an LDM we need to eliminate the many-to-many relationships.

The most common method for doing this is to create a new entity, called an **associative entity**. It is put it in the middle with the primary keys of the two tables on either side as foreign keys. For this new associative entity, we will need a good primary key. We can do this in three ways:

1. concatenate the foreign keys to become a compound primary key,
2. choose another attribute to use as the primary key, or
3. add a surrogate key and use it as the primary key.

In the parts/order/customer example, we will create an associative table named 'orderdetail'. This new table will have the part_id and order_id as foreign keys connecting back to part and order entities. The quantity of a part on an order will be an attribute on that new table. Finally, we will concatenate the part_id and order_id together into a compound key and use it as the primary key. With the compound key, each part/order combination has only one quantity. It would also have been correct to add a surrogate key to the 'orderdetail' and to have part_id and order_id as regular attributes and foreign keys.

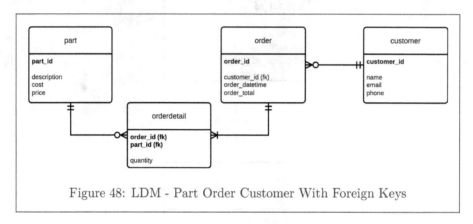

Figure 48: LDM - Part Order Customer With Foreign Keys

This diagram may now be read as: 1) a customer has zero or more orders and an order is placed by only one customer; 2) an order has one or more order details and an order detail can only be part of a single order; and 3) a part may be on several order details, but an order detail may only have one part.

Another Example

Let us look at another example. An automobile insurance policy may have several drivers and several cars listed on it. The CDM might look something like:

56

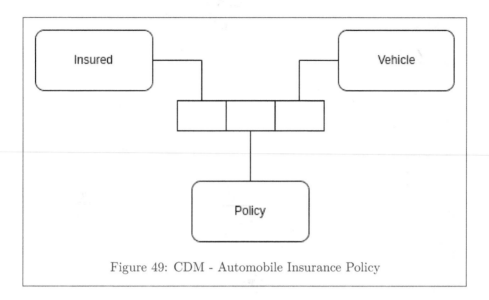

Figure 49: CDM - Automobile Insurance Policy

In this example, a vehicle may be on zero or many policies and an insured may be on zero or more policies. A policy must have at least one insured and vehicle. The crows foot LDM with many-to-many relationships would look like:

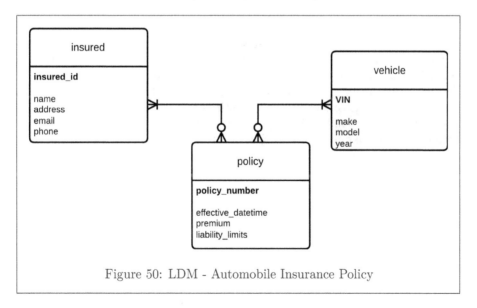

Figure 50: LDM - Automobile Insurance Policy

The model with many-to-many relationships does not have specific information like coverage levels for vehicles (which may be different for each one) or what roles an insured has within the policy. To model these additional pieces of data, we would create associative entities and implement the primary keys of the insured, vehicle, or policy entities as foreign keys on the new tables.

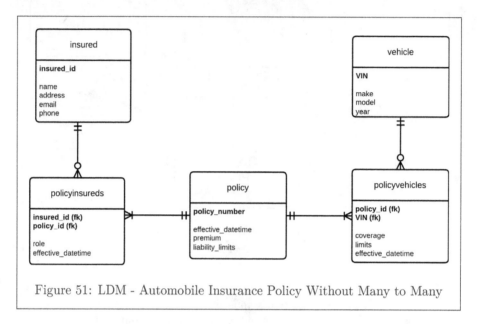

Figure 51: LDM - Automobile Insurance Policy Without Many to Many

Specialization Hierarchy in an ERD

In the discussion of the CDM, we saw that entities may share common properties or be derived from a more general entity. We call this specialization or generalization of entities a specialization hierarchy. We use the words "is a" or "has a" to describe generalization and specialization. These relationships come in two types: inclusive and exclusive. Entities in an inclusive relationship may have zero or more (multiple) specializations. With an exclusive relationship an entity may only be one of type of specialization.

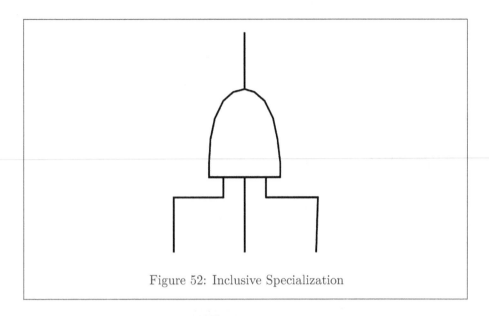

Figure 52: Inclusive Specialization

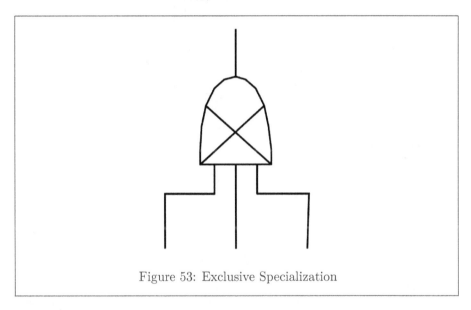

Figure 53: Exclusive Specialization

The Entity Relationship Diagram (ERD) introduces two new symbols to show these type of relationship: 1) the inclusive specialization shown by a symbol with a rounded top and a flat bottom and 2) the exclusive specialization is the same symbol but with an added "X". Typically the generalization, or parent' is connected with a straight line to the top of the symbol and the children are connected with lines from the bottom.[29]

[29]Erwin. (2020). Data Modeling Overview - IDEF1X and IE Subtype Notation. Retrieved

The specialized entities usually share the same primary key as the general entity. Because they share the same key, data may be retrieved from the various tables with ease.

This is an example of a inclusive specialization hierarchy. A person may be a customer and a vendor, or an employee and a donor. Actually in most situations a person may be a combination any or all of the four types.

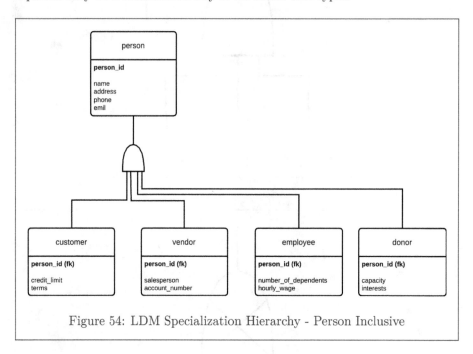

Figure 54: LDM Specialization Hierarchy - Person Inclusive

The second specialization hierarchy example describes the situation that a person may own zero or more vehicles. Vehicles come in various types (specializations), like: automobile, truck, or motorcycle. We can see in the ERD that there are many common attributes between all types of vehicles (generalization) and that the subtypes all have their own unique attributes. This relationship is exclusive because a vehicle can't be both a car and a truck.

The diagram also included labels on the subtype relationships that specify the vehicle type. On the general entity (vehicle) the vehicle_type attribute will contain an "A", "T", or "M" that specifies which specialization exists. The vehicle_type attribute may also be NULL denoting that no specialization has been defined.

https://tinyurl.com/bdehmt8r

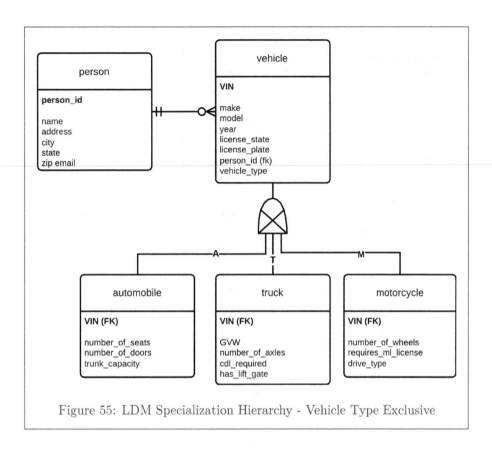

Figure 55: LDM Specialization Hierarchy - Vehicle Type Exclusive

Case One - Neighborhood Bodega

Consider the neighborhood bodega we looked at in the previous chapters. We have identified entities, attributes, and keys. It is now time to finish the Logical Data Model (LDM/ERD) by adding our foreign keys and identifying our relationships.

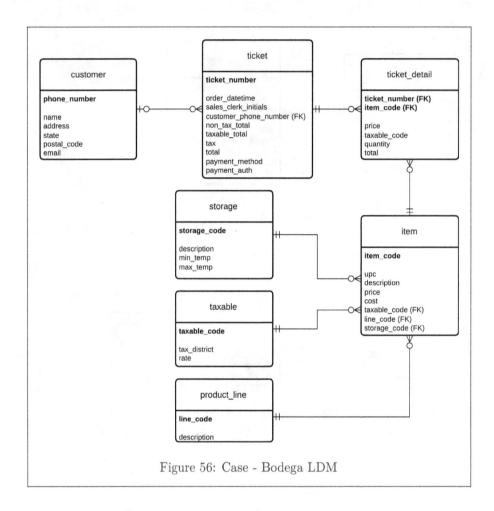

Figure 56: Case - Bodega LDM

If there had been significant differences in types of items or of customers, we may need to create a subtype relationship.

Case Two - Sensor Readings

If we split out the sensor specific information into separate entities, we develop an LDM like:

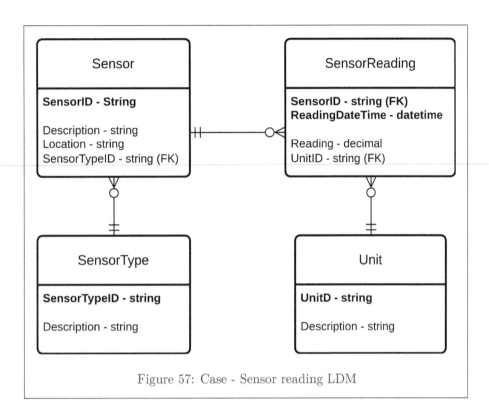

Figure 57: Case - Sensor reading LDM

Exercises

1. Draw a crows-foot ERD for the following scenario. Be sure to include primary keys, foreign keys, and a few attributes.

   A company has many departments and employees. An employee is assigned to a single department as their 'home' and a department has several employees. Each employee is either a 'member' or a 'manager' of their department. An employee has a primary key of their employee_number and the department has the primary key of department_id.

2. Draw a crows-foot ERD for the following scenario. Be sure to include primary keys, foreign keys, and a few attributes.

   A bakery has many customers that it delivers to on a weekly basis. The territory is broken into routes and each customer belongs to a single route. A route may have one or more customers. A driver may be assigned more than one route and all routes must have one driver.

This page intentionally left blank.

Chapter 7 - SQL Selecting Data

This chapter will allow you to see what tables exist in a database and introduce how to retrieve data from those tables using Structured Query Language (SQL). We will see in later chapters how to limit our searches to specific rows, how to summarize data, and how to perform simple calculations. In this chapter, we will be using the VetOffice demo database.

Examples and assignments in the SQL chapters will use several different sample relational databases. These databases are listed with descriptions and ERDs in the Appendix. Downloads of the SQL files to create the databases are also provided and can be found at https://www.learn2db.com.

Before doing any SQL, you must be first connected to a database or database server through a piece of client software.

Objectives

At the conclusion of this lesson module, students will be able to:

1. understand the difference in various database implementations handling the quoting of strings and identifiers.
2. understand the case-sensitivity of identifiers and SQL language elements when using different database implementations on different operating systems.
3. be able to list the tables that exist on the specific database they are using.
4. be able to quote strings and expressions for the specific database they are using.
5. write **SELECT** statements to show all columns of a table.
6. use **SELECT** to limit the columns displayed to specific ones.

SQL Statement Conventions Used in This Book

Case sensitivity (capital vs. lower case letters) of identifiers and the use of quotes around strings and identifiers may vary across specific database implementations. To make the examples, work for most databases with the default configuration, the following capitalization and quotation standard will be used in SQL statements in the text of this book:

- SQL Keywords (like **SELECT**, **WHERE**, and **JOIN**) will be capitalized so that they stand out.
- Identifiers (like database, table, and column names) will usually be shown in snake case or all in lower case.[30] Snake case uses only lower case letters with underscores (_) between words. Examples include: some_data, number_of_people, last_name, invoice_total, transactiondetail, quantitysold, and number_of_students.

---

[30] https://developer.mozilla.org/en-US/docs/Glossary/Snake_case

- Strings will be in single quotes (').

  Examples include: 'Bob''s Car', 'Any "thing"', '9956%^ty', and '2024-10-13'

Case-Sensitivity and Quotes

What is Case-Sensitivity?

Many programming languages are case-sensitive (upper and lower case letters are different).[31] In the SQL language, the language keywords are case-insensitive (can be upper, lower, or mixed) but the names of the tables and columns may be case-sensitive ('Customer' may not be 'customer').

Quotes

If you have a string value to insert or use in your SQL statements, you will need to put that value in quotation marks. You may also see column and table names, often called identifiers quoted, when they contain special names or have names that conflict with SQL keywords.

The ANSI SQL standard uses single quotes (') around strings of text, like: names, addresses, and other data values ('jim', '123 main street', 'P.O. box 765', 'B747-300'). If you need a single quote inside a string, just double it ('John''big boy" Smith').

The standard also says that you can use double quotes (") around identifiers in your SQL statement. This is not the default behavior in MySQL and MariaDB.

MySQL and MariaDB

Case Sensitivity

The default case sensitivity depends upon the Operating System: - Windows and macOS, table and column names are case-insensitive. - For most LINUX systems, table and column names are case-sensitive (very common for Web servers).

Strings – Data

- Single quotces (') [32]

  ```
  'foo'
  'bar'
  'something "cool".'
  ```
- Double quotes (")

  ```
  "Jim's Stuff"
  "foofoo"
  "abc123"
  ```

---

[31] https://learnsql.com/blog/sql-case-sensitive/
[32] https://dev.mysql.com/doc/refman/8.0/en/string-literals.html

Identifiers (Table and Column names)

- Back ticks (`) [33]

```
SELECT `colname`
FROM sometable;
```

SQLite

Case Sensitivity

Column and table names are case-insensitive. Database specific statements, like '.tables' and '.quit', are case-sensitive (they must be in lower case).

Strings – Data

- Single quotes (') - Use two single quotes inside string if your string contains a single quote.

```
'a string'
'Jim''s string'
```

Identifiers (Table and Column names)

- Double quotes (") [34]

```
SELECT "colname" FROM "sometable";
```

- Back ticks (`)

```
SELECT `colname` FROM sometable;
```

- Square Brackets ([])

```
SELECT * FROM [sometable];
```

MSSQL Server

Case Sensitivity

Column and table names are case-insensitive.

Strings – Data

- Single quotes (')

```
'name of something'
'something "else".'
```

---

[33] https://dev.mysql.com/doc/refman/8.0/en/identifiers.html
[34] https://sqlite.org/lang_keywords.html

Identifiers (Table and Column names)

- Double quotes (") [35]

  ```
  SELECT "colname" FROM "sometable";
  ```

- Square Brackets ([])

  ```
  SELECT * FROM [sometable];
  ```

This setting can be changed to follow the ANSI Standard with the `QUOTED_IDENTIFIER` option.[36]

Listing Tables

If you are opening up a new database or one that you don't have completely committed to memory, it is helpful to see what tables exist. Many of us will be connecting through a graphical or Web interface that will show what tables exist and the columns that have been defined. For those of us who are connecting using a **command line interface** (CLI), each database vendor has their own way to do this, as it was not part of the original SQL standard.

MySQL and MariaDB

```
SHOW TABLES;
```

Table 37: Tables in VetOffice Database

Tables_in_vetoffice
animal
gender
owner
species

SQLite

```
.tables
```

```
animal gender owner species
```

MSSQL Server

```
SELECT table_name, table_schema
 FROM information_schema.tables
 ORDER BY table_name ASC;
```

---

[35] https://learn.microsoft.com/en-us/sql/relational-databases/databases/database-identifiers?view=sql-server-ver16

[36] https://learn.microsoft.com/en-us/sql/t-sql/statements/set-quoted-identifier-transact-sql?view=sql-server-ver16

table_name	table_schema
animal	dbo
gender	dbo
owner	dbo
species	dbo

Selecting All Rows and Columns

The SELECT statement allows you to pull and summarize data from your database. It returns a **recordset** of rows and columns of data. You can think of it like a Swiss Army Knife with dozens of options, clauses, and an infinite functionality.

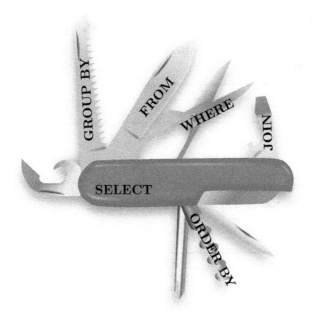

The first use of the SELECT statement simply tells the database to return all columns and all rows from the table as a recordset.

Statement	Description
SELECT * FROM table;	Return all columns and rows of a table as a recordset.

Example

```
SELECT * FROM owner;
```

Table 40: Select All Rows from Owner Table

owner_id	last_name	first_name	phone	email
1	Smithson	Amy	1-555-555-3467	asmit89@notreal.com
2	Ralston	Howard	1-555-555-6712	howie88@notreal.com
3	Greene	Susan	1-555-555-5543	catwoman@notreal.com
4	Luton	Lex	1-555-555-9988	lexlex@notreal.com
5	Clark	John	1-555-555-8111	johnnyc@notreal.com

If you wanted to look at the data in the other tables, just change the name after FROM to the table you wish to view.

Selecting Individual and Specific Columns

To see specific columns, replace the * in our SELECT statement with a comma separated list of column names.

Statement	Description
SELECT column_name or expression, ... FROM table;	Return specified columns or calculations from a table as a recordset.

Example

For example, if we just want to see email addresses and the names of the owners.

```
SELECT email, last_name, first_name FROM owner;
```

Table 42: Select Specific Columns from Owner Table

email	last_name	first_name
asmit89@notreal.com	Smithson	Amy
howie88@notreal.com	Ralston	Howard
catwoman@notreal.com	Greene	Susan
lexlex@notreal.com	Luton	Lex
johnnyc@notreal.com	Clark	John

Case

Using the Media Collection sample data we will ask a few questions and get the answers using SELECT. Because some of the recordsets will be large, the results shown may have some of the rows replaced with ellipses.

Show all artists in the database.

```
SELECT * FROM artist;
```

Table 43: Select all columns and rows from the artist table.

artist_id	name
1	Motley Grunge
2	Queen Ant
3	Roach to Men
4	Taylor Slow
5	George Wiggly
6	Madison Tuckered
7	Purple Frog
8	Hazy Daisy
9	Frankie Ford Cooper
10	Stanberg Cubic
999	Various

Show all the album titles.

```
SELECT album_title FROM album;
```

album_title
Motley as it Gets
Motley and More
Can't Get More Motley
Echoes of Stardust
Midnight Mirage
...
Greatest Hits of the Century

Exercises

For this chapter's exercises, use the Toy Store Order sample database.

1. Write a query to show all the items that we sell at the store.
2. Write a query to show item id, name, and price from the items table.

This page intentionally left blank.

Chapter 8 - Arithmetic Operators, Selected Numeric Functions and Aliasing a Column

SQL has many functions and operators to perform calculations with numbers. This chapter will show many common operators and functions that deal with numbers. In addition to the numeric operations, this chapter will show how to change the name of a column or calculation in a recordset and do some basic formatting.

Each SQL implementation should have all the functions covered in this chapter, but may have several more. Be sure to look at the specific system documentation for additional functions and features.

Many of the SQL examples in this chapter will use a form of the **SELECT** statement without a **FROM** clause. This allows us to experiment with expressions without using a table and will return one row of results. In the expressions where constant numbers are used, column names or other expressions may be used as you use these techniques with real data.

Objectives

At the conclusion of this lesson module, students will be able to:

1. perform arithmetic with constants and attributes.
2. use integer division and calculate the remainder/modulo.
3. use the ROUND function to limit number of decimal places shown in a query.
4. use the AS clause to create an alias for a column or an expression.
5. convert floating point values to whole numbers by rounding, finding the floor or finding the ceiling.
6. Use power and logarithmic functions.

Arithmetic Operators

The six arithmetic operators of addition, subtraction, multiplication, division, and modulo follow the same order of operations that they do in other common uses. Multiplication, division, and modulus are completed first and then addition and subtraction are done. The order may be changed by grouping your expression using parenthesis.

Table 45: Arithmetic Operators on SQL

Operator	Description
expr1 + expr2	Addition
expr1 - expr2	Subtraction
expr1 * expr2	Multiplication

Operator	Description
expr1 / expr2	Division (See below for details)
expr1 % expr2	Modulus
(expression)	Order of Operation

Addition, Subtraction and Multiplication

Example

Show the results of 7 times 9 plus 3, and 7 times the quantity 15 minus 3.

```
SELECT 7 * 9 + 3, 7 * ( 15 - 3 );
```

Table 46: Simple Arithmetic

7 * 9 + 3	7 * (15 - 3)
66	84

Division

There are some differences in databases regarding how division is handled using the / operator.

MySQL and MariaDB

The MySQL and MariaDB databases will always return a floating point number when performing division using the / operator. MySQL adds an additional operator DIV to specifically perform integer division that discards the decimal part.[37]

Table 47: MySQL Division Operators

Operator	Description
expr1 / expr2	Floating Point Division
expr1 DIV expr2	Integer Division (returns a whole number of times the divisor goes into the dividend)

Example

```
SELECT 6/5, 6 DIV 5, 6.0/5, 6/5.0, 6.0/5.0;
```

---

[37]https://dev.mysql.com/doc/refman/8.4/en/arithmetic-functions.html#operator_divide

Table 48: Division - MySql and MariaDB

6/5	6 DIV 5	6.0/5	6/5.0	6.0/5.0
1.2000	1	1.20000	1.2000	1.20000

SQLite and MSSQL Server

With SQLite and MSSQL Server if both the divisor and dividend are integers then the result will also be an integer, and the decimal part will be discarded.[38] If either or both of the numbers are floating point numbers, then the result will also be a floating point number.

When dividing two integers and a floating point result is desired, you may need to multiply one of them by 1.0 or casting them to a different type.

Example

```
SELECT 6/5, 6/(5*1.0), 6.0/5, 6/5.0, 6.0/5.0;
```

Table 49: Division - SQLite and MSSQL Server

6/5	6/(5*1.0)	6.0/5	6/5.0	6.0/5.0
1	1.2	1.2	1.2	1.2

Example

For an example of division, we might want to show animals with their weight in kilograms (KG) when the attribute data is currently stored as pounds. By dividing by 2.2 we can convert from one to the other.

```
SELECT name, weight / 2.2, species_id
    FROM animal;
```

Table 50: Animal Weights in KG

name	weight / 2.2	species_id
Kitty	7.72727272727273	C
Bobo	10.4545454545455	D
Daisy	3.18181818181818	C
Bonnie	4.09090909090909	C
Cookie	5.45454545454545	C
Cookie	5.45454545454545	D

---

[38]https://learn.microsoft.com/en-us/sql/t-sql/language-elements/divide-transact-sql?view=sql-server-ver16

name	weight / 2.2	species_id
Penny	6.81818181818182	C
Holly	1.81818181818182	C
Rosie	2.27272727272727	C

Modulus Operator

When we were first learning long division, we were calculating the modulus but we called it the remainder.

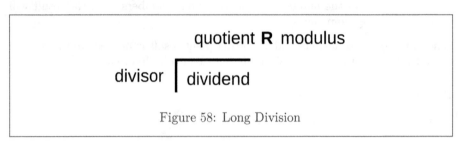

Figure 58: Long Division

In SQL, the % operator is used to calculate the reminder of division of two numbers.[39] [40] The modulus operator comes in useful when splitting values apart for reporting, like when calculating hours, minutes and seconds from seconds. It also has many uses in data science.

Example

Let us look at a small example of modulus at work. Our veterinarian wants to split customers into 3 groups for performing A-B testing of a marketing email. The three groups are 0-get nothing, 1-get email A, and 2-get email B. We can use the modulus operator on the sequentially assigned customer number to get the group number, whenever we want.

```
SELECT owner_id, last_name, first_name, owner_id % 3
    FROM owner;
```

Table 51: Modulus Example

owner_id	last_name	first_name	owner_id % 3
1	Smithson	Amy	1
2	Ralston	Howard	2
3	Greene	Susan	0

[39] https://dev.mysql.com/doc/refman/8.4/en/mathematical-functions.html#function_mod

[40] https://learn.microsoft.com/en-us/sql/t-sql/language-elements/modulo-transact-sql?view=sql-server-ver16

owner_id	last_name	first_name	owner_id % 3
4	Luton	Lex	1
5	Clark	John	2

Aliasing a Column

In the division example above, you should notice that the column name returned, in the recordset, is either the string '(No column name)' (in MSSQL) or the expression used. We may create a column alias using the AS clause. The alias will be displayed as the column name and can be used in other clauses of the statement.

Example

Assign a meaningful column name to the weight in KG expression.

```
SELECT name, weight / 2.2 AS kg, species_id AS species
    FROM animal;
```

Table 52: Animal Weights in KG with Column Alias

name	kg	species
Kitty	7.72727272727273	C
Bobo	10.4545454545455	D
Daisy	3.18181818181818	C
Bonnie	4.09090909090909	C
Cookie	5.45454545454545	C
Cookie	5.45454545454545	D
Penny	6.81818181818182	C
Holly	1.81818181818182	C
Rosie	2.27272727272727	C

Rounding Your Results

When we are performing operations with numbers, we often get results with too many decimal places. These extra digits returned are often confusing and add no accuracy to the results. The ROUND function takes a floating point expression and rounds it to a whole number or to a specific number of decimal places.

MySQL, MariaDB, and MSSQL Server

MySQL, MariaDB, and MSSQL Server support a ROUND() function that will round a number on either side of the decimal places. If the length is positive, it will round to that many decimal places. Otherwise, if the length is negative, it will round on the whole number side. Lastly, if the length is zero (or omitted on MySQL) it will round to a whole number.[41] [42]

A number of the same type will be returned. If you are rounding a decimal number, a decimal will be returned even if you are rounding to a whole number.

Table 53: MySQL and MSSQL Round Function

Function	Description
ROUND(expr, n)	Round a number to the number of specified decimal places.

Example

Round a number to zero, one, and two decimal places. Also round the number to the tens place.

```
SELECT ROUND(135.13579,0) AS R0,
    ROUND(135.13579,1) AS R1,
    ROUND(135.13579,2) AS R2,
    ROUND(135.13579,-1) AS Rn1;
```

Table 54: Rounding Examples - MySQL, MariaDB, and MSSQL Server

R0	R1	R2	Rn1
135.0	135.1	135.14	140

SQLite

SQLite's ROUND() function will round on the decimal side with a 0 or positive length, but will not support a negative length. Additionally, SQLite always returns a decimal number even if you are rounding an integer.[43]

Table 55: SQLite Round Function

Function	Description
ROUND(expr)	Round a number to no decimal places.

---

[41] https://dev.mysql.com/doc/refman/8.4/en/mathematical-functions.html#function_round
[42] https://learn.microsoft.com/en-us/sql/t-sql/functions/round-transact-sql?view=sql-server-ver16
[43] https://www.sqlite.org/lang_corefunc.html#round

Function	Description
ROUND(expr, n)	Round a number to the number of specified decimal places.

Example

Round a number to zero, one, two, and 3 decimal places.

```
SELECT ROUND(12.345678) AS R,
    ROUND(12.345678,0) AS R0,
    ROUND(12.345678,1) AS R1,
    ROUND(12.345678,2) AS R2,
    ROUND(12.345678,3) AS R3;
```

Table 56: Rounding Examples - SQLite

R	R0	R1	R2	R3
12.0	12.0	12.3	12.35	12.346

Example

If we take our animal weight in KG example to the next step, we can now round the result to a reasonable number of decimal places.

```
SELECT name, ROUND(weight / 2.2, 1) AS kg, species_id
    FROM animal
    ORDER BY kg;
```

Table 57: Animal Weights in KG with Column Alias and Rounding

name	kg	species_id
Holly	1.8	C
Rosie	2.3	C
Daisy	3.2	C
Bonnie	4.1	C
Cookie	5.5	C
Cookie	5.5	D
Penny	6.8	C
Kitty	7.7	C
Bobo	10.5	D

Other Decimal to Whole Number Functions

Often, when working with numeric values, the difference between an integer and a decimal (floating point number) is not an issue. Problems arise when we are counting discrete things like people or products. We will want to use an exact integer value and not a decimal number for many of our calculations. The following functions convert a decimal to the closest integer.[44] [45] [46]

Table 58: Functions to Truncate Decimal Fraction

Function	Description
CEILING(expr)	Find the next greater or equal integer.
FLOOR(expr)	Find the closest lesser or equal integer.

Example

Display the floor and ceiling of different decimal numbers.

```
SELECT CEILING(2.9) AS C2_9, FLOOR(2.9) AS F2_9,
    CEILING(-1.5) AS Cn1_5, FLOOR(-1.5) AS Fn1_5,
    CEILING(9.0) AS C9, FLOOR(9.0) AS F9;
```

C2_9	F2_9	Cn1_5	Fn1_5	C9	F9
3.0	2.0	-1.0	-2.0	9.0	9.0

Logarithmic and Power Functions

Logarithms and powers are used to calculate compound interest, measure earthquakes (Richter Scale), study atomic decay (half-life), describe growth, and many other things.

Raising a Value to a Power

The first of these functions we will cover is the POWER() function. It takes one number (base) and raises it to another (exponent).

Table 60: Power Function

Function	Description
POWER(base, exponent)	Raise the number represented by base to the exponent power.

---

[44] https://learn.microsoft.com/en-us/sql/t-sql/functions/ceiling-transact-sql?view=sql-server-ver16

[45] https://dev.mysql.com/doc/refman/8.4/en/mathematical-functions.html#function_ceiling

[46] https://www.sqlite.org/lang_mathfunc.html#floor

Example

As an example of the POWER function let us take a list of investments and their expected interest rates to calculate the final value of each of these investments. This calculation is known as the future value and the formula is:

$$ fv = pv * (1 + i)^n $$

Figure 59: Future Value Formula

Our sample data looks like:

invest_id	description	start_datetime	amount	years	rate
1	Growth-O-Matic	2024-08-01 12:15	100000.0	5.0	0.094
2	Loan to B, Smith	2024-08-22 16:24	1000.0	1.0	0.135
3	Mega Loss Enterprises	2024-08-15 09:01	34000.0	2.0	-0.1
4	Short Term Loan to Z. Broz	2024-08-30	1356.0	0.083	0.23

To calculate the future value (FV) of money invested, we could calculate it like:

```
SELECT invest_id, amount AS PV,
    ROUND(amount * POWER( 1 + rate , years ),2) AS FV
    FROM invest;
```

invest_id	PV	FV
1	100000.0	156706.36
2	1000.0	1135.0
3	34000.0	27540.0
4	1356.0	1379.5

Exponential Value

The EXP() function raises the base of the natural logarithm (e, approx: 2.71828) to the specified power. It is the opposite of LN() function.[47]

For many, the mathematical constant 'e', the base of the natural logarithm, is quite a mystery. It simply is the result of 1 unit over 1 time unit being continuously compounded at 100%. To restate, think about the scenario where we have $1 and the bank will give us 100% interest, how much will we have in

---

[47]https://learn.microsoft.com/en-us/sql/t-sql/functions/exp-transact-sql?view=sql-server-ver16

a year. Different number of compounds will give us different answers. In the formula below, as 'n' approaches infinity the result is 'e'.

$$\left(1 + \frac{1}{n}\right)^n$$

Figure 60: Compound Interest Formula

n	Value in a Year
1	2.0
2	2.25
4	2.44140625
12	2.613035290224676
365	2.7145674820219727
infinity	2.718281828459045

Table 64: Exp Function

Function	Description
EXP(expression)	Return the exponential value of expression.

Example

```
SELECT EXP(1), EXP(2.89), EXP(LN(10));
```

Table 65: EXP Function - Output

EXP(1)	EXP(2.89)	EXP(LN(10))
2.71828182845905	17.9933096015503	10.0

Natural Logarithm

The natural logarithm is the opposite of the `EXP()` function. It takes a number and finds the exponent that we need to raise 'e' to. [48]

---

[48] https://learn.microsoft.com/en-us/sql/t-sql/functions/log-transact-sql?view=sql-server-ver16

Table 66: Natural Logarithm Function

Function	Description
LN(base)	Calculate the natural logarithm of the number base.

Example

```
SELECT LN(2.7), LN(18);
```

Table 67: LN Function - Output

LN(2.7)	LN(18)
0.993251773010283	2.89037175789616

Base 10 Logarithm

In some instances, we may need to calculate the logarithm of a number in base 10 and not in the natural base 'e'. We use the LOG() function to do this. It is the opposite operation of raising an exponent to the power of 10 , like POW(10, exp).

Table 68: Base Ten Logarithm Function

Function	Description
LOG(exp)	Calculate the base 10 logarithm.

Example

```
SELECT LOG(2.7), LOG(10010929);
```

Table 69: LOG Function - Output

LOG(2.7)	LOG(10010929)
0.431363764158987	7.00047438126082

Exercises

For these problems, use the Music Collection database.

1. Using the Music Collection database, list movie titles with their length broken into three columns (hours, minutes, and seconds).

2. We are interested in selling off our movies. List movie titles with their cost, cost plus 50% as the minimum we will accept, and 275% of cost as the price we will list them for. There is one we have already sold but still list it. Put nice names on the calculated columns and round to 2 decimal places.

3. List album's title, price, cost, profit made from selling them, and lastly markup. Put nice names on the calculated columns and show markup as rounded whole percent.

Chapter 9 - SQL Limiting Rows

In a previous chapter, we have seen the use of the general `SELECT` statement to return a listing of all the rows in a table. The `WHERE` clause is used in the `SELECT` and `UPDATE` statements to limit the number of rows.

Objectives

At the conclusion of this lesson module, students will be able to:

1. use the `WHERE` clause to limit the recordset.
2. create complex Boolean expressions using `AND`, `OR`, and `NOT`.
3. use the comparison operators to compare expressions.
4. create and use the `LIKE` operator with wildcard expressions to match parts of an expression.

Comparison Operators

Before we an begin to select individual rows or groups of rows from a table, we need to start by showing how to make comparisons. The comparison operators allow us to compare two expressions.[49] [50] In MSSQL Server, the return values will be true or false. The return value will be `1` or `0` in the other databases.

Table 70: SQL Comparison Operators

Comparison Operator	Description
expr1 = expr2	Equal To
expr1 <> expr2	Not Equal To
expr1 != expr2	Not Equal To
expr1 < expr2	Less Than
expr1 <= expr2	Less Than or Equal
expr1 > expr2	Greater Than
expr1 >= expr2	Greater Than or Equal

With these comparison operators we can compare columns to constant values, to each other, or even to complex expressions. In this chapter, we will keep it simple.

Example

---

[49] https://learn.microsoft.com/en-us/sql/t-sql/language-elements/comparison-operators-transact-sql?view=sql-server-ver16

[50] https://www.sqlite.org/lang_expr.html#operators_and_parse_affecting_attributes

Table 71: Comparisons and Their Result

Expression	SQLite and MySQL	MSSQL
5 = 5	1	true
8 < 5	0	false
5 <= 6	1	true
5 >= 6	0	false
5 <> 5	0	false
'Joe' = 'Jones'	0	false
'apple' <= 'peach'	1	true

Where - Limit Rows

The WHERE clause allows us to limit our recordset to the specific rows that we want. We need to create an expression that will evaluate to a true value for the rows we want. Rows with a false value will not be included.

Clause	Description
WHERE boolean_expression	Include row when expression evaluates to true.

Example

In the following statements, we will see the use of the WHERE clause with a comparison of a column to a value. The first example shows a list of all Dogs, where species_id is equal to 'D'.

```
SELECT name, owner_id, color, weight FROM animal
 WHERE species_id = 'D';
```

Table 73: Select with Simple Where

name	owner_id	color	weight
Bobo	1	Brown	23.0
Cookie	4	Light Brown	12.0

The second example we have a sale on Flea Drops for animals weighing 10 or less pounds.

```
SELECT owner_id, name, death_datetime, weight
    FROM animal
    WHERE weight <= 10;
```

Table 74: Another Select with Simple Where

owner_id	name	death_datetime	weight
3	Daisy	NULL	7.0
3	Bonnie	2024-04-03 15:39	9.0
5	Holly	NULL	4.0
5	Rosie	NULL	5.0

Wildcard Comparison Operator

Sometimes we only know part of an attribute's value, like an incomplete phone number or email address, and still want to select the records that match the partial criteria. We call this type of query a "Wildcard" query. It uses the special LIKE operator.

Table 75: Like Operator

Operator	Description
expr LIKE searchExpr	Return true if expression matches the wildcard search expression otherwise false.

Using multi-character wildcard:

- string% - Match with expressions starting with string.
- %string - Match with expressions ending in string.
- %string% - Match with expressions containing string anywhere.
- st%ng - Match an expression that starts with 'st' and ends with 'ng'.

Using a single-character wildcard:

- L_ndon - Match London, Lyndon, Landon, or any six letter expression starting with 'l' and ending with 'ndon'.

The LIKE operator makes a comparison ignoring the case of letters. It takes a special string expression containing % to match groups of zero or more characters and _ to match one character. Some SQL implementations may add additional functionality, but this should work in most variants.

Example

For example, we can make out the last four digits of an owners phone number from a scribbled message left to us taped to the door and it looks like 9988. We can find the owner with:

```
SELECT * FROM owner WHERE phone LIKE '%9988';
```

Table 76: Select with Wildcard

owner_id	last_name	first_name	phone	email
4	Luton	Lex	1-555-555-9988	lexlex@notreal.com

NULL Values

Modern relational databases have a special value, called `NULL`, that represents a value that has no value. This may seem rather unusual, but is it? For example, what if we have a table of employees with various values and one of the columns is number_of_children. The value of zero may be a correct value, so what should we store if we do not know? This is where `NULL` comes in.

In the VetOffice database, we can see the `NULL` value used in the death_datetime column of the animal table. If the animal is alive, then the death_datetime is unknown.

Because `NULL` represents nothing, anything compared to `NULL` is always `NULL`.

Example

Table 77: Comparing Values with NULL

Expression	Result
`1 = NULL`	`NULL`
`99 <> NULL`	`NULL`
`'jim' < NULL`	`NULL`
`NULL = NULL`	`NULL`
`NULL <> NULL`	`NULL`

NULL Comparison Operators

The special operators `IS` and `IS NOT` are included in SQL to allow for testing if a value is `NULL`. The `IS NULL` operator will return a true value if a cell is `NULL` and false if the cell contains a value (even zero or an empty string). The `IS NOT NULL` operator will do the opposite.

Operator	Description
`expr IS NULL`	True if data value is `NULL`.
`expr IS NOT NULL`	True if data value is not `NULL`.

Example

Display a list of living animals.

```
SELECT owner_id, name, species_id, animal_id
    FROM animal
    WHERE death_datetime IS NULL;
```

owner_id	name	species_id	animal_id
1	Kitty	C	1
3	Daisy	C	3
3	Cookie	C	5
4	Cookie	D	6
5	Penny	C	7
5	Holly	C	8
5	Rosie	C	9

Logical Operations

The operators of conjunction (AND), disjunction (OR) and negation (NOT) were described and standardized in a book by George Boole in 1847 as he was studying the algebra of true and false values.[51] Boolean Algebra, the study of true and false values, bears his name in honor of his contributions. We regularly use the words and, or, and not as we communicate with each-other, but sometimes we are not as exact as we need to be when dealing with a database query.

Operator	Description
expr1 AND expr2	Conjunction – true if both are true.
expr1 OR expr2	Disjunction – true if either are true.
NOT expr	Negation - Switch true to false and false to true.

The logical operators AND and OR are both associative and commutative, like multiplication and addition.[52] In a logical expression, NOT is evaluated first, then AND, and finally OR. Parenthesis may be added to a logical expression to add clarity and to ensure that the operations are handled in the correct order. You may also use the distributive property of AND over OR to simplify expressions.

In a relational database the logic of the three Boolean operators change slightly because of the special nature of the NULL value. Remember any operation (logical, arithmetic, and comparison) involving NULL will always return NULL or an error.

---

[51] https://www.gutenberg.org/ebooks/36884

[52] The NROC Project. (N.D.) Libre Texts - Applied Mathematics / Developmental Math - 9.3.1: Associative, Commutative, and Distributive Properties. Retrieved https://tinyurl.com/5aznt3tc

And

AND	TRUE	FALSE
TRUE	TRUE	FALSE
FALSE	FALSE	FALSE

Or

OR	TRUE	FALSE
TRUE	TRUE	TRUE
FALSE	TRUE	FALSE

Not

NOT	
TRUE	**FALSE**
FALSE	TRUE

Examples

In this example, we are looking for all the dogs that are alive. To do this, we need to select for the animals that do not have a death date and with a species_id equal to 'D'.

```
SELECT animal_id, owner_id, name, color
    FROM animal
    WHERE death_datetime IS NULL AND species_id = 'D';
```

animal_id	owner_id	name	color
6	4	Cookie	Light Brown

In another example, we have a new food to help owners to keep their 'fat' cats on a diet without starving them. The veterinarian has defined a cat weighing 15 pounds or more is a good candidate for this product.

```
SELECT animal_id, owner_id, name, weight
    FROM animal
    WHERE species_id = 'C' AND weight >= 15;
```

animal_id	owner_id	name	weight
1	1	Kitty	17.0
7	5	Penny	15.0

Case

You have been asked by the owner of the toy store a series of questions, and you need to answer them with queries from the Toy Store Orders sample database.

The first question they asked was to create a list of customers with 'john' somewhere in their name. Include their customer number, name, city, state, and country.

```
SELECT customer_id, name, city, state_id, country_id
FROM customer
WHERE name LIKE '%john%';
```

customer_id	name	city	state_id	country_id
13	Kenneth Johnson	Wadsworth	OH	US
69	Suzanne Johnson	Mount Laurel	NJ	US
110	John Thompson	Wyoming	MI	US

The owner was pleased with your results and wants to do some geographical marketing. In the United States, the first three digits of a zip code define a geographical region of several post offices, called a commercial zone. Can you create a list of all customers in the area around Yuma AZ (85365) showing name, email, city, and postal-code?

```
SELECT customer_id, name, city, state_id
FROM customer
WHERE postal_code like '853%' AND country_id = 'US';
```

Table 87: Customers in Commercial Zone 853

customer_id	name	city	state_id
14	Debra Lloyd	Sun City	AZ
68	Terry Mckinney	Glendale	AZ
75	Chelsea Graves	Yuma	AZ
100	Kristin Kline	Yuma	AZ
117	Dalton Acosta	Yuma	AZ
127	Tiffany Silva	Glendale	AZ

The owner would like to see the "corporate" customers. The easiest way to do this is to show the customers who do not pay their own invoice, but have the invoice sent to another party. The billto_customer_id would not be NULL for these customers. Just show the customer ID, their name, and the number of the customer getting the bill.

```
SELECT customer_id, name, billto_customer_id
FROM customer
WHERE billto_customer_id IS NOT NULL;
```

customer_id	name	billto_customer_id
18	Mega Big Box Store 101	10
29	Toys-r-cool Store 99	12
47	Toys-r-cool Store 555	12
64	Mega Big Box Store 501	10
65	Mega Big Box Store 523	10
66	Mega Big Box Store 574	10
113	Toys-r-cool Store 42	12
131	Mega Big Box Store 555	10

Exercises

For this chapter's exercises, use the Media Collection sample database.

1. Use **SELECT** to create a list of albums by artist #7 "Purple Frog".
2. The 1980s were totally 'rad' and the first half was the best musically, some think. List all albums made between 1980 and 1984.
3. Create a list of albums by artist #4 "Taylor Slow" that she created in the 1970s.
4. List all albums with 'dream' in their title.

Chapter 10 - SQL Order Matters

A relational database may store and retrieve the rows of a table in a random or apparent random order, unless you specify how you want them sorted. Some databases store rows in the order they were added, but the default order cannot be guaranteed. To get the results of a SELECT in the order you wish, you need to add the ORDER BY clause.

Objectives

At the conclusion of this lesson module, students will be able to:

1. sort a recordset in ascending order.
2. sort using one or more columns.
3. sort by expression in descending order.
4. sort a recordset in random order.

Adding Order

We can add the ORDER BY clause at the end of the SELECT statement followed by one or more column names or expressions. The recordset will be sorted by the first column, and then with each of the following columns. By default, the sort order is ascending (going from smallest to largest). For numeric columns, the data will be sorted numerically. String columns (even if the fields contain a number) they will be sorted alphabetically. And date and time columns will be sorted in date order (the oldest date first).

Clause	Description
ORDER BY expression, ...	Sort the recordset in order by the expression or expressions.

Sorting with a Single Column

If we follow the ORDER BY clause with a single column name or expression, the recordset will be ordered by that expression. When there are multiple columns with the same value, then the order of those columns in the group is undetermined.

Example

In this example, we want to order our owners by their balance.

```
SELECT *
    FROM ownerbalance
    ORDER BY balance;
```

owner_id	balance
1	123.45
3	345.98

Sorting with Multiple Columns

You may specify multiple column names or expressions in your `ORDER BY` clause. This will cause the database to sort by the first one and then by the subsequent ones.

Example

In this example we sort first by species, then by gender within species, then by name within gender and species.

```
SELECT name, species_id, gender_id
    FROM animal
    ORDER BY species_id, gender_id, name;
```

name	species_id	gender_id
Holly	C	F
Rosie	C	M
Bonnie	C	NF
Daisy	C	NF
Penny	C	NF
Cookie	C	NM
Kitty	C	NM
Cookie	D	NF
Bobo	D	NM

Turning the Sort Order Around

Sort order may be changed to descending order (largest to smallest) on an individual column or expression basis. Simply add the `DESC` keyword after the column name or expression in the `ORDER BY` clause and that column will be in descending order.

Example

Our veterinarian would like to sort living animals by species and then by age, with the youngest first.

```
SELECT name, species_id, birth_datetime, owner_id
    FROM animal
    WHERE death_datetime IS NULL
    ORDER BY species_id, birth_datetime DESC;
```

name	species_id	birth_datetime	owner_id
Daisy	C	2021-07-10	3
Holly	C	2021-06-12	5
Rosie	C	2021-06-12	5
Kitty	C	2020-01-23	1
Cookie	C	2019-01-30 06:15	3
Penny	C	2018-07-07	5
Cookie	D	2020-11-11	4

Random Order

Sometimes, we want our recordset to be returned in a random order. All of our databases have functionality to generate pseudo-random numbers. When we use a random number as the expression in the `ORDER BY` clause, we will mix up the rows.

Pseudo-random numbers appear to be random but are actually created by a deterministic algorithm that can generate the same sequence if the seed (starting) value is the same.[53] Their properties are used in simulations and cryptography to repeat a process that acts random. By default the seeds are randomized so you get a different sequence each time you run a statement.

MySQL, MariaDB, and MSSQL Server

In MySQL, MariaDB, and MSSQL Server, the function to generate random numbers is `RAND()`.[54] [55] It will return a random floating point number greater than or equal to zero and always less than 1.

Table 93: Rand function in MySQL and MSSQL

Function	Description
RAND()	Return a pseudo-random decimal where 0 <= n < 1.

Example

```
SELECT animal_id, name, owner_id
    FROM animal
    WHERE death_datetime IS NULL
    ORDER BY RAND();
```

---

[53] https://en.wikipedia.org/wiki/Pseudorandomness

[54] https://dev.mysql.com/doc/refman/8.4/en/mathematical-functions.html#function_rand

[55] https://learn.microsoft.com/en-us/sql/t-sql/functions/rand-transact-sql?view=sql-server-ver16

animal_id	name	owner_id
9	Rosie	5
7	Penny	5
6	Cookie	4
8	Holly	5
5	Cookie	3
1	Kitty	1
3	Daisy	3

SQLite

In SQLite, the RANDOM() function returns an pseudo-random 64bit signed integer value between -9223372036854775808 and +9223372036854775807. [56]

Table 95: Random function in SQLite

Function	Description
RANDOM()	Return a pseudo-random integer between -9223372036854775808 and +9223372036854775807.

Example

```
SELECT owner_id, last_name, first_name
    FROM owner
    ORDER BY RANDOM();
```

owner_id	last_name	first_name
2	Ralston	Howard
3	Greene	Susan
5	Clark	John
4	Luton	Lex
1	Smithson	Amy

Case

We will return to the Toy Store Order database for a few additional.

List the customers from New York ('NY') showing their postal code, name, and email address in postal code order, then in alphabetical order by name.

---

[56]https://www.sqlite.org/lang_corefunc.html#random

```
SELECT postal_code, name, email
   FROM customer
   WHERE state_id = 'NY'
   ORDER BY postal_code, name;
```

postal_code	name	email
11365	Tanya Gregory	tanya5371@foo.bar
11413	Kayla Welch	kayla3646@yahfoo.bogus
11420	Alejandro Edwards	aleja7939@demofoo.bogus
11420	Amy Frank	amyfr6279@demofoo.bogus
11420	Elizabeth Gonzales	eliza4657@gfake.bogus
11432	Gina Fowler	ginaf7932@gfake.bogus
11758	Thomas Contreras	thoma2612@demostuff.bogus
11791	Ashley Butler	ashle6139@demofoo.bogus
13023	Miss Ashley Hahn	missa2389@foo.bar
14424	Michael Cuevas	micha5554@demofoo.bogus

One more. A customer wants to get a gift for their nibbling and wants to spend not more than $15.00. Show the name and price of items with a price between $5 and $15 in descending order by price.

```
SELECT description, price
   FROM item
   WHERE price >= 5 AND price <= 15
   ORDER BY price DESC;
```

description	price
Giant Wooden Yo-Yo	13.67
Rainbow Flying Disk	8.98
Blue Flying Disk	7.89
Red Flying Disk	7.89
Yo-Yo Wax	6.67

Exercises

For this chapter's exercises, use the Media Collection sample database.

1. List the albums by 'George Wiggly' (artist #5) in alphabetical order by title.

2. List all albums by 'Purple Frog' (artist #7) in descending order by release year then alphabetically by title within the year.

3. List all songs that have a title starting with the letter 'A' in alphabetical order by their title.

This page intentionally left blank.

Chapter 11 - Normalization and the Physical Data Model

Normalization is the process of taking user data, identifying entities and relationships from it, and developing a good data model from it. For most business needs, data normalized to the third normal form (3NF) is sufficient to create a good database structure with a limited amount of redundant data. There are higher levels of normalization that are beyond the scope of this work.

Objectives

At the conclusion of this chapter, students will be able to:

1. define and describe the first three forms of normal data.
2. create data in First Normal Form (1NF).
3. take data that is in 1NF and remove the partial dependencies to create in the Second Normal Form (2NF).
4. develop data to the Third Normal Form (3NF).
5. use the 3NF definition to model to draw a Physical Data Model.

First Normal Form (1NF)

First normal form is all about getting the data into a single entity that we may store in a database. As a single table, there will usually be redundant data making maintenance difficult and storage inefficient.

In first normal form (1NF), we need to take the user's data and:

1. eliminate repeating groups of data,
2. split attributes into their atomic (smallest) parts, and
3. define a good primary key.

When we successfully do these three things, then each row will be:

1. unique, and
2. order of rows and columns will not change the meaning of the data.

In this chapter, we have been given a meeting listing for a society called the Data Modelers Association and have been asked to create a good data model. To help explain the data, they have also told us a few facts:

- A group may meet many times a week at one or more locations.
- A location may only have one meeting going at once.

Table 99: Un-normalized Data Modelers Association club schedule

meeting day	meeting time	group	location	comments
Friday	19:00	102 - Diagramming Demons	DEQ - Data Equipment 707 Landings Place Seattle WA 90876	
Monday	12:00	102 - Diagramming Demons	ICBM - Intergalactic Computer Business Machines 123 Main St Topeka KS 67890	Lunch Provided
	19:00	103 - Kitbashers Klick	AZ - Amazzing Hosting 222 NOVA Center Arlington VA 23922	

meeting day	meeting time	group	location	comments
		101 - Midnight Modelers	ICBM - Intergalactic Computer Business Machines 123 Main St Topeka KS 67890	
Saturday	08:00	103 - Kitbashers Klick	DEQ - Data Equipment 707 Landings Place Seattle WA 90876	Beginner Meeting
Wednesday	19:00	101 - Midnight Modelers	ICBM - Intergalactic Computer Business Machines 123 Main St Topeka KS 67890	

The spreadsheet above was given to you by the master modeler with the groups and their meetings. The first step is to remove the repeating groups. If we look at the data, there are three meetings on Monday and even two meetings at 7PM on Monday. The repeating field was probably left off for readability. We just repeat the missing data so that every row has all the data it needs to be understood without another row.

Table 100: Data Modelers Association club schedule without repeating groups.

meeting day	meeting time	group	location	comments
Friday	19:00	102 - Diagramming Demons	DEQ - Data Equipment 707 Landings Place Seattle WA 90876	
Monday	12:00	102 - Diagramming Demons	ICBM - Intergalactic Computer Business Machines 123 Main St Topeka KS 67890	Lunch Provided
Monday	19:00	103 - Kitbashers Klick	AZ - Amazzing Hosting 222 NOVA Center Arlington VA 23922	
Monday	19:00	101 - Midnight Modelers	ICBM - Intergalactic Computer Business Machines 123 Main St Topeka KS 67890	
Saturday	08:00	103 - Kitbashers Klick	DEQ - Data Equipment 707 Landings Place Seattle WA 90876	Beginner Meeting
Wednesday	19:00	101 - Midnight Modelers	ICBM - Intergalactic Computer Business Machines 123 Main St Topeka KS 67890	

Now that we have eliminated the repeating groups, we can look for columns that contain multiple values of different types. These non-atomic columns need broken into their distinct pieces.

- Split the group column into separate columns for the
  - group ID and
  - another for the name.
- Split the location column into new columns for the:
  - location ID,
  - name,
  - address,
  - city,
  - state, and
  - postal code.

Once this is accomplished all the columns will be atomic (they only contain one data value).

meeting day	meeting time	group id	group name	location id	location name	address	city	state	zip	comments
Friday	19:00	102	Diagramming Demons	DEQ	Data Equipment	707 Landings Place	Seattle	WA	90876	

meeting day	meeting time	group id	group name	location id	location name	address	city	state	zip	comments
Monday	12:00	102	Diagramming Demons	ICBM	Intergalactic Computer Business Machines	123 Main St	Topeka	KS	67890	Lunch Provided
Monday	19:00	103	Kitbashers Klick	AZ	Amazzing Hosting	222 NOVA Center	Arlington	VA	23922	
Monday	19:00	101	Midnight Modelers	ICBM	Intergalactic Computer Business Machines	123 Main St	Topeka	KS	67890	
Saturday	08:00	103	Kitbashers Klick	DEQ	Data Equipment	707 Landings Place	Seattle	WA	90876	Beginner Meeting
Wednesday	19:00	101	Midnight Modelers	ICBM	Intergalactic Computer Business Machines	123 Main St	Topeka	KS	67890	

To fully get this data into 1NF, we need to identify a primary key so that we can store the data into the database as a single entity. At this point, we can create a composite key by concatenating attributes together, or we can assign a surrogate key as the primary key.

A good composite key for the data would be group_id, meeting_day, and meeting_time. This will allow different groups to meet at the same time and a group to potentially meet twice on the same day or at the same time on different days. Below you will see a relational diagram that shows that all the fields are dependent upon the primary key.

In a relational diagram, the columns are assigned to boxes, parts of the primary key are highlighted, and arrows are drawn representing the parts of the composite key, if applicable, and the fields that are based on the key.

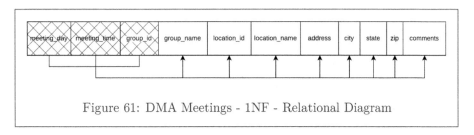

Figure 61: DMA Meetings - 1NF - Relational Diagram

We are in 1NF. The data can go into a database table and be queried using SQL.

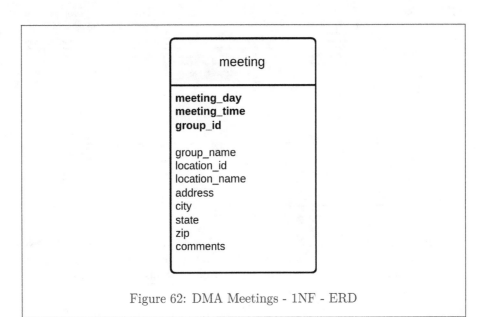

Figure 62: DMA Meetings - 1NF - ERD

Second Normal Form (2NF)

In second normal form (2NF), we will identify and split out the redundant data that is based upon part of the primary key, known as a **partial dependency**. This will reduce some of the duplicated data by creating new entities. If we used a single attribute or a surrogate key (simple key) for the primary key in 1NF, then our data is already in 2NF.

In second normal form (2NF) we:

1. take the structure from 1NF, and
2. identify partial dependencies, and
3. move the partial dependencies to their own table.

Partial Dependency

A partial dependency is created when a data field is dependent upon part, but not all, of a composite primary key.[57] Looking at the data, we can see that the group_name is dependent upon the group_number and the meeting date and time do not affect the group_name. We can show that in our dependency diagram.

---

[57]https://www.javatpoint.com/partial-dependency-in-dbms

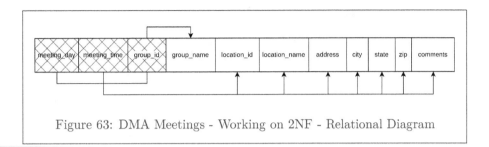

Figure 63: DMA Meetings - Working on 2NF - Relational Diagram

Now that we have identified the partial dependency of group_name and group_id, we can split it off into a separate table/entity.

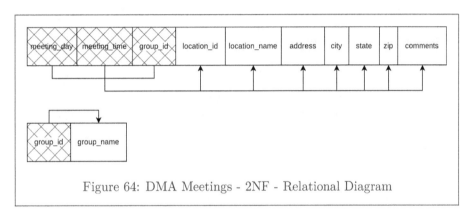

Figure 64: DMA Meetings - 2NF - Relational Diagram

There are no more dependencies so we are now in 2NF.

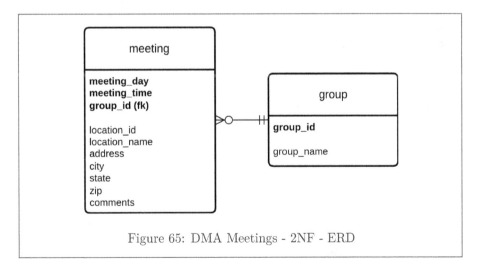

Figure 65: DMA Meetings - 2NF - ERD

Third Normal Form (3NF)

Now that we have normalized the data to 2NF, we need to continue looking for columns that may be related to other columns in the data. These attributes would not be related directly to the primary key or part of the primary key.

In third normal form (3NF) we:

1. take the structure from 2NF, and
2. identify transitive dependencies, and
3. move the transitive dependencies to their own table.

Transitive Dependency

A transitive dependency is created when a data field is dependent on a field that is not part of the primary key.[58] Sometimes we will have fields that are related, but we will not have a good identifier (primary key) for those fields. We may need to add a surrogate key to the table we are creating and also add that key, as a foreign key, to the table we are splitting these fields from.

Looking at the data, we can see that the location name, address, city, state, and zip are dependent upon the location_id and not the entire primary key. This is a transitive relation.

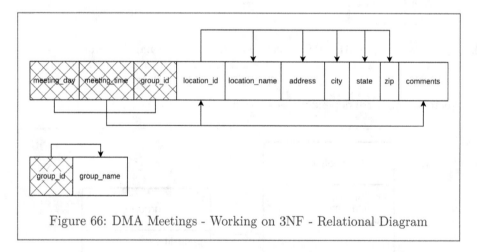

Figure 66: DMA Meetings - Working on 3NF - Relational Diagram

We have identified the transitive dependency. There is one, location. We can now split it into a new table.

---

[58] https://www.sciencedirect.com/topics/computer-science/transitive-dependency

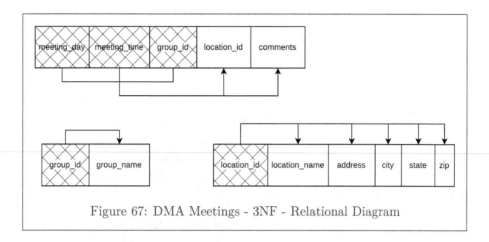

Figure 67: DMA Meetings - 3NF - Relational Diagram

We are now in 3NF.

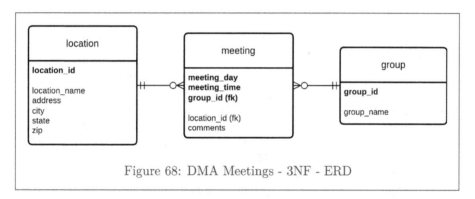

Figure 68: DMA Meetings - 3NF - ERD

Higher Order Forms

There are further definitions of higher order and more stringent normal forms. The next normal mode, known as Boyce-Codd (BCNF or 3.5NF) is a stricter version of 3NF where all redundancies in data are removed. There are also higher forms, but they are beyond the coverage of this text.

Case

This case represents a small board game manufacturer's games and the parts that make up each game. The data includes game ids, part ids, cost for each part, quantity needed of each part in a game, and the retail price of a complete game. Below is the spreadsheet of games given to you by the owner of the company. We need to normalize this data into 3NF.

game	retail price	parts cost quantity
fz Fab Zuper	29.95	d6 6 Sided Die 0.25 4
		fzb Fab Zuper Board 5.25 1
		fzi Fab Zuper Instructions 0.76 1
		rck Rubber Chicken 3.87 1
fzd Fab Zuper Deluxe	59.99	d6 6 Sided Die 0.25 4
		fzb Fab Zuper Board 5.25 1
		fzi Fab Zuper Instructions 0.76 1
		fzlf Fab Zuper Leather Folio 20.98 1
		rck Rubber Chicken 3.87 2
rfz Revenge of Fab Zuper	39.99	d6 6 Sided Die 0.25 8
		fzi Fab Zuper Instructions 0.76 1
		rck Rubber Chicken 3.87 4
		rfzb Fab Revenge Board 5.25 1

1NF

First step will be to get rid of the repeating groups. We will split each part to its own line and repeat the other columns.

game	retail price	parts cost quantity
fz Fab Zuper	29.95	d6 6 Sided Die 0.25 4
fz Fab Zuper	29.95	fzb Fab Zuper Board 5.25 1
fz Fab Zuper	29.95	fzi Fab Zuper Instructions 0.76 1
fz Fab Zuper	29.95	rck Rubber Chicken 3.87 1
fzd Fab Zuper Deluxe	59.99	d6 6 Sided Die 0.25 4
fzd Fab Zuper Deluxe	59.99	fzb Fab Zuper Board 5.25 1
fzd Fab Zuper Deluxe	59.99	fzi Fab Zuper Instructions 0.76 1
fzd Fab Zuper Deluxe	59.99	fzlf Fab Zuper Leather Folio 20.98 1
fzd Fab Zuper Deluxe	59.99	rck Rubber Chicken 3.87 2
rfz Revenge of Fab Zuper	39.99	d6 6 Sided Die 0.25 8
rfz Revenge of Fab Zuper	39.99	fzi Fab Zuper Instructions 0.76 1
rfz Revenge of Fab Zuper	39.99	rck Rubber Chicken 3.87 4
rfz Revenge of Fab Zuper	39.99	rfzb Fab Revenge Board 5.25 1

Second step will be to break the non-atomic attributes into separate columns.

game id	game name	retail price	part id	part name	part cost	quantity
fz	Fab Zuper	29.95	d6	6 Sided Die	0.25	4
fz	Fab Zuper	29.95	fzb	Fab Zuper Board	5.25	1

game id	game name	retail price	part id	part name	part cost	quantity
fz	Fab Zuper	29.95	fzi	Fab Zuper Instructions	0.76	1
fz	Fab Zuper	29.95	rck	Rubber Chicken	3.87	1
fzd	Fab Zuper Deluxe	59.99	d6	6 Sided Die	0.25	4
fzd	Fab Zuper Deluxe	59.99	fzb	Fab Zuper Board	5.25	1
fzd	Fab Zuper Deluxe	59.99	fzi	Fab Zuper Instructions	0.76	1
fzd	Fab Zuper Deluxe	59.99	fzlf	Fab Zuper Leather Folio	20.98	1
fzd	Fab Zuper Deluxe	59.99	rck	Rubber Chicken	3.87	2
rfz	Revenge of Fab Zuper	39.99	d6	6 Sided Die	0.25	8
rfz	Revenge of Fab Zuper	39.99	fzi	Fab Zuper Instructions	0.76	1
rfz	Revenge of Fab Zuper	39.99	rck	Rubber Chicken	3.87	4
rfz	Revenge of Fab Zuper	39.99	rfzb	Fab Revenge Board	5.25	1

If we select game_id concatenated with part_id as a compound primary key, we have the following relational diagram. The data is in 1NF.

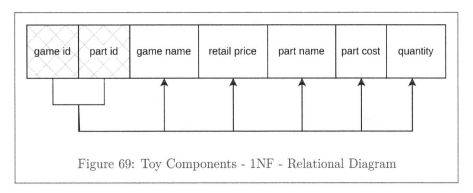

Figure 69: Toy Components - 1NF - Relational Diagram

2NF

As we examine the relational diagram for the 1NF solution, we will see a couple of different partial dependencies. The game name and retail price are dependent only on the game id. The part name and part cost are only dependent on the part id. Quantity is dependent on game and part. Otherwise we couldn't have different parts or quantity of a part on different games.

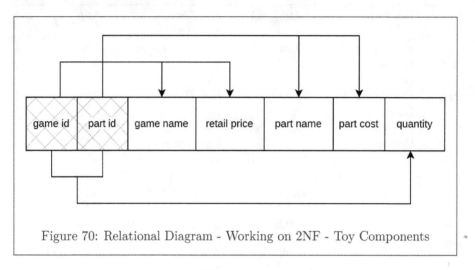

Figure 70: Relational Diagram - Working on 2NF - Toy Components

Now split into three separate entities:

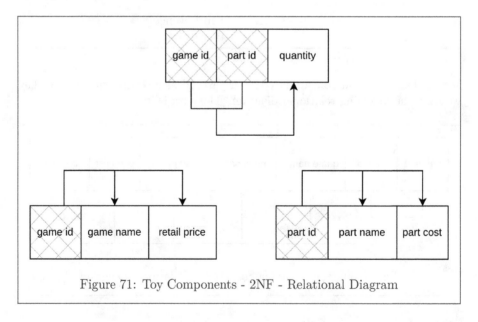

Figure 71: Toy Components - 2NF - Relational Diagram

We are now in 2NF.

3NF

There are no transitive dependencies, so no additional changes need to me made. 3NF is the same as 2NF. We can redraw this as an ERD:

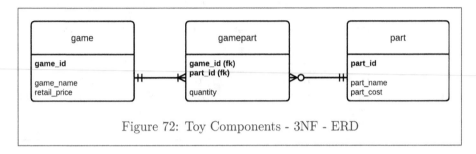

Figure 72: Toy Components - 3NF - ERD

Exercises

1. You have been given a spreadsheet of artists and paintings that they have done by a curator at a local art gallery. Please normalize the data to 3NF.

   The Accession Number represents the year that we acquired the piece and the order within the year (001 - first, 002 - second...).

Accession Number	Artist	Born-Died	Artist From	Painting	Year	Value
2023-001	Leonardo Jones	1650-1710	Naples Italy	Big Boat	1682	1000000
2022-027				Small Green Boat	1687	500000
2022-029				Sketch of Ear	1709	250000
2022-001	Claude Smith	1880-1930	Paris France	Dead Water Lillies	1922	333334
2022-017				Boat in Cattails	1927	333334

1. You have a list of printer cartridges and the model numbers of the printers that they fit. Some cartridges may fit in several printers, and some printers will use more than one cartridge. Normalize this to 3NF so that we can search by cartridge or by printer model.

109

Cart Manufacturer	Cart Number	Cart Description	Color	Printer Models
Hewlet Pacific	H56	Ink Jet	Black	HP1934, HP4563, HP7856
	H56H	Ink Jet - High Capacity	Black	HP4563, HP7856
	H99C	Ink Jet	Cyan	HP9901, HP 9910
	H99Y	Ink Jet	Yellow	HP9901, HP 9910
Crawford	CF88	Lazer	Black	CF1000, CF100, CF200, CF300
	CF77	Lazer	Black	CF1000, CF100

110

Chapter 12 - SQL Joining Tables

In the data normalization chapter, we split most of the redundant data into separate tables to reduce the difficulty of maintenance and to reduce storage. For example, we moved customer names and addresses to a separate customer table. The `JOIN` clause will allow us to bring those tables back together and extract fields from multiple tables in a single query.

Objectives

At the conclusion of this lesson module, students will be able to:

1. use an inner join to connect tables together in a single query.
2. develop outer joins to connect tables where some columns might not have corresponding values.

The Inner Join

The `INNER JOIN` is the most commonly used join by developers. It will extract the rows where the primary and foreign keys match. If there are NULL values or values that may not exist on the other side of the join, then the row will not be included.

In SQL, the order of the clauses is important. The `JOIN` clause should follow the `FROM` clause directly and come before `WHERE`, `ORDER BY`, and several other clauses we will learn about.[59] [60]

After the table name the key word `ON` is followed by a Boolean expression describing the relationship between the two tables. Usually it is the name of the foreign key column tested for equality with the primary key of the other table.

If columns exist with the same name on the tables in a join, SQL will require us to put the table name (or table alias) with a dot before the column name. This removes the possible confusion of which table to extract the value from.

Table 107: Inner Join Clause

SQL Clause	Description
`JOIN source ON expression`	Perform an inner Join on the criteria.
`INNER JOIN source ON expression`	With optional `INNER` keyword

---

[59] https://www.sqlite.org/syntax/join-clause.html
[60] https://dev.mysql.com/doc/refman/8.4/en/join.html

Examples

For our first example, let us create a listing of animals with their owners. We want to see the animal information and owner ID number, and name. We're going to have to join the animal and the owner tables to do this.

We have to include the table name with the column names, in the ON clause, separated by a dot. Both tables contain a field called owner_id, so just using owner_id alone is ambiguous. SQL doesn't know which attribute from which table you want to use.

```
SELECT animal_id, name, species_id, owner.owner_id,
    last_name, first_name
    FROM animal
    JOIN owner ON animal.owner_id = owner.owner_id;
```

Table 108: Animal Owner Inner Join

animal_id	name	species_id	owner_id	last_name	first_name
1	Kitty	C	1	Smithson	Amy
2	Bobo	D	1	Smithson	Amy
3	Daisy	C	3	Greene	Susan
4	Bonnie	C	3	Greene	Susan
5	Cookie	C	3	Greene	Susan
6	Cookie	D	4	Luton	Lex
7	Penny	C	5	Clark	John
8	Holly	C	5	Clark	John
9	Rosie	C	5	Clark	John

What if we now wanted a list of species with the description of the species and the animals that belong to the species, and for the animals we would like see animal_id, name, and color?

```
SELECT species.species_id, description,
    animal_id, name, color
    FROM species
    JOIN animal
        ON species.species_id = animal.species_id
    ORDER BY species.species_id, name;
```

Table 109: Species Animal Inner Join

species_id	description	animal_id	name	color
C	Feline	4	Bonnie	Black
C	Feline	5	Cookie	Ginger
C	Feline	3	Daisy	Callico

species_id	description	animal_id	name	color
C	Feline	8	Holly	Black
C	Feline	1	Kitty	Ginger
C	Feline	7	Penny	Ginger
C	Feline	9	Rosie	Black
D	Canine	2	Bobo	Brown
D	Canine	6	Cookie	Light Brown

If we select the species table and view all the rows, we will see that not all the rows were returned. Only the rows that matched the criteria in the ON clause were returned.

The Outer Join

In an OUTER JOIN, all the rows from one table and the corresponding rows from the other table will be included. When using a LEFT OUTER JOIN, the table whose name is on the left side of the expression will be completely included. The right side table may have all of its rows included with a RIGHT OUTER JOIN.

Because you cannot do a right or left inner join, the word OUTER is optional and automatically assumed when you say RIGHT JOIN or LEFT JOIN.

Table 110: Outer Join Clauses

SQL Clause	Description
LEFT OUTER JOIN source ON expression	Perform a left outer Join on the criteria.
LEFT JOIN source ON expression	Without Optional OUTER keyword.
RIGHT OUTER JOIN source ON expression	Perform a right outer Join on the criteria.
RIGHT JOIN source ON expression	Without Optional OUTER keyword.

Examples

We are going to take one of the previous examples and change it into an OUTER JOIN. By saying 'species LEFT OUTER JOIN animal' we will get ALL species, even if there is not a match, and all of the animals that match.

```
SELECT species.species_id, description,
    animal_id, name, color
    FROM species
    LEFT OUTER JOIN animal
        ON species.species_id = animal.species_id
    ORDER BY species.species_id, name;
```

Table 111: Species Animal Left Outer Join

species_id	description	animal_id	name	color
C	Feline	4	Bonnie	Black
C	Feline	5	Cookie	Ginger
C	Feline	3	Daisy	Callico
C	Feline	8	Holly	Black
C	Feline	1	Kitty	Ginger
C	Feline	7	Penny	Ginger
C	Feline	9	Rosie	Black
D	Canine	2	Bobo	Brown
D	Canine	6	Cookie	Light Brown
H	Equine	NULL	NULL	NULL

By switching the order of the table names we can write an equivalent query using a RIGHT JOIN.

```
SELECT species.species_id, description,
    animal_id, name, color
    FROM animal RIGHT
    JOIN species
        ON species.species_id = animal.species_id
    ORDER BY species.species_id, name;
```

Table 112: Species Animal Left Outer Join

species_id	description	animal_id	name	color
C	Feline	4	Bonnie	Black
C	Feline	5	Cookie	Ginger
C	Feline	3	Daisy	Callico
C	Feline	8	Holly	Black
C	Feline	1	Kitty	Ginger
C	Feline	7	Penny	Ginger
C	Feline	9	Rosie	Black
D	Canine	2	Bobo	Brown
D	Canine	6	Cookie	Light Brown
H	Equine	NULL	NULL	NULL

Join a Table to Itself

In a unary relationship, a table references itself. If we need to join a table to itself, we need to use the AS clause on the JOIN so that we can differentiate between the two instances of the same table. Doing this type of JOIN is often called a **recursive join** or **self join**.

114

Clause	Description
`JOIN table AS alias`	Assign an alias name to a table in a join

Example

In this example, we have a table containing members of an exclusive club. After the initial people became members, new members need to be referred by another member.

The data looks like:

member_id	member_name	expire_datetime	referred_member_id
JR	James Reneau	2025-12-31 23:59	NULL
VD	Vinnie Davis	2025-12-31 23:59	NULL
AC	Amy Covington	2024-12-31 23:59	JR
PJ	Patricia Jones	2023-12-31 23:59	JR
LL	Larry Leftwitch	2027-12-31 23:59	AC
NT	Nancy Townes	2025-12-31 23:59	LL

The ERD for the single recursive table is:

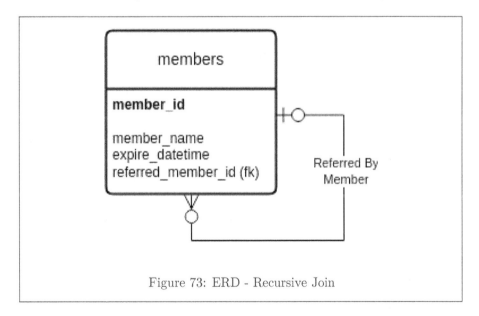

Figure 73: ERD - Recursive Join

You can see in the ERD that the members table has a reference back to itself. What if we wanted to see a list of all members, and who referred them? The following statement would do the trick. Pay attention to how the `AS` clause has created an alias for the second occurrence of the members table.

115

```
SELECT members.member_id, members.member_name,
    ref.member_id AS referred_by_id,
    ref.member_name AS referred_by_name
    FROM members
    LEFT JOIN members AS ref
        ON members.referred_member_id = ref.member_id
    ORDER BY members.member_id;
```

member_id	member_name	referred_by_id	referred_by_name
AC	Amy Covington	JR	James Reneau
JR	James Reneau	NULL	NULL
LL	Larry Leftwitch	AC	Amy Covington
NT	Nancy Townes	LL	Larry Leftwitch
PJ	Patricia Jones	JR	James Reneau
VD	Vinnie Davis	NULL	NULL

Other Joins

There are two other types of joins you may see in your coding: 1) the FULL OUTER JOIN and 2) the CROSS JOIN.

The Full Outer Join

FULL JOIN brings rows from both tables with or without a match. Think of it as a right outer join plus the unmatched rows from a left outer join.

MYSQL does not support this clause.

Table 115: Full Outer Join Clauses

SQL Clause	Description
FULL OUTER JOIN source ON expression	Perform a full outer Join on the criteria.
FULL JOIN source ON expression	

The Cross Join

The CROSS JOIN or , (comma) join creates a Cartesian Product. A **Cartesian Product** of two tables is every row of the first table repeated with every row of the second table. If the first table contained 100 rows and the second table contained 20 rows, then the result would be 2000 rows. This gets very large, very quickly.

With a CROSS JOIN the INNER JOIN may be created using the WHERE clause and selecting the matching rows. It is not suggested that you do this because you are bypassing SQL's optimisations and this will use a lot of resources.

Examples

A nonsense example would be the cross product of the gender and species table. But it does show ALL of the possible combinations of the two.

```
SELECT *
   FROM gender, species;
```

gender_id	description	species_id	description
M	Male	C	Feline
M	Male	D	Canine
M	Male	H	Equine
NM	Neutered Male	C	Feline
NM	Neutered Male	D	Canine
NM	Neutered Male	H	Equine
F	Female	C	Feline
F	Female	D	Canine
F	Female	H	Equine
NF	Neutered Female	C	Feline
NF	Neutered Female	D	Canine
NF	Neutered Female	H	Equine
U	Unknown	C	Feline
U	Unknown	D	Canine
U	Unknown	H	Equine

A typical **INNER JOIN** can be rewritten as a cross join. It is not recommended but it would look like:

```
SELECT species.species_id, description,
   animal_id, name, color
   FROM species, animal
   WHERE species.species_id = animal.species_id
   ORDER BY species.species_id, name;
```

species_id	description	animal_id	name	color
C	Feline	4	Bonnie	Black
C	Feline	5	Cookie	Ginger
C	Feline	3	Daisy	Callico
C	Feline	8	Holly	Black
C	Feline	1	Kitty	Ginger
C	Feline	7	Penny	Ginger
C	Feline	9	Rosie	Black
D	Canine	2	Bobo	Brown
D	Canine	6	Cookie	Light Brown

Case

Using the Media Collection database, we know the song title contains the word 'cosmic' and we want to see those songs, original artist, albums, and the album artist for songs with that title. We will need to join multiple tables and even join the artist table twice to do this.

```
SELECT song.song_title, artist.name AS artist,
album.album_title, album_artist.name AS AlbumArtist
FROM song
LEFT JOIN artist
ON song.artist_id = artist.artist_id
LEFT JOIN album_track
ON album_track.song_id = song.song_id
LEFT JOIN album
ON album_track.album_id = album.album_id
LEFT JOIN artist AS album_artist
ON album_artist.artist_id = album.artist_id
WHERE song_title LIKE '%cosmic%';
```

song_title	artist	album_title	AlbumArtist
Cosmic Carousel	George Wiggly	Crimson Cascade	George Wiggly
Cosmic Canticle	George Wiggly	Galactic Groove	George Wiggly
Cosmic Crescendo	George Wiggly	Lunar Lullaby	George Wiggly
Cosmic Canticle	Motley Grunge	Motley and More	Motley Grunge
Cosmic Canticle	Motley Grunge	Best Of	Motley Grunge

Exercises

Answer the following with queries from the Toy Store Orders sample database.

1. Please show a list of order headers from customers in Florida ('FL'). Show customer name, city, order id, data, and total. Sort by order datetime.

2. Create a listing of items on order 1030. Show item id, item, name, qty ordered, price, and extended price (quantity times price). Be sure to sort by item id.

3. Create a listing of vendors and the items that they supply. Include vendor id, name, email, item id, description, and price. Order by vendor name then the item description.

4. Modify the previous select to show ALL vendors, even the ones with no items.

5. Create a listing of customers who have their bills sent to another customer (with billto_customer_id). This list needs to show the customer id and name of the original customer, and the customer id, name, and email

address of the customer that invoices should be sent to. Order by bill to customer number then by customer number.)

This page intentionally left blank.

Chapter 13 - SQL Aggregate Functions

So far we have extracted data from a table and limited the result to specific rows and columns. While this detail is helpful, we sometimes need to aggregate it into a total, count the rows, calculate the mean, or find the largest or smallest value.

Objectives

At the conclusion of this lesson module, students will be able to:

1. count number of rows in a recordset.
2. total and calculate the mean of a numeric value in a recordset.
3. find the minimum and maximum value of an expression in a recordset.
4. concatenate values from multiple rows in a recordset as a single value.

Counting Rows

The COUNT() function will count non-NULL rows in a recordset. You may use a * for the expression to return the total number of rows.

Table 119: Count Function

Function	Description
COUNT(expr)	Return the count of the non-NULL values.

Example

Count the total number of animals and the number of deceased animals (ones with a deceased date).

```
SELECT COUNT(*) as NumberOfAnimals,
    COUNT(death_datetime) as DeceasedCount
    FROM animal;
```

NumberOfAnimals	DeceasedCount
9	2

Calculating Totals

To calculate the total of numeric fields, we can use the SUM() function.

Table 121: Sum Function

Function	Description
SUM(expr)	Return the total of a numeric expression.

Example

Our veterinarian wants a quick answer of how much they are owed. We just do a quick summation of the balance.

```
SELECT SUM(balance) as TotalOutstanding
    FROM ownerbalance;
```

TotalOutstanding
469.43

Calculating Average Value (Mean)

We could use the SUM() and COUNT() functions to calculate the mean value, but SQL includes a function to do it for us. Use the AVG() function to return the mean value of a numeric expression.

Table 123: Avg Function

Function	Description
AVG(expr)	Return the mean of a numeric expression.

Example

Our veterinarian would like to know the average weight of all cats in the database.

```
SELECT AVG(weight) as AverageCat
    FROM animal
    WHERE species_id = 'C';
```

AverageCat
9.85714285714286

Finding the Minimum and Maximum Values

We can also use the MIN() and MAX() functions to find the minimum and maximum values of an expression. You are not limited to finding the minimum and maximum of numeric values, `MIN()` and `MAX()` can be found for all data types.

Table 125: Min and Max Functions

Function	Description
MIN(expr)	Return the minimum value of an expression.
MAX(expr)	Return the maximum value of an expression.

Example

Our veterinarian has decided they also need to know the smallest and largest cat based on weight. Again they are not concerned with if they are living or deceased.

```
SELECT MIN(weight) as SmallestCat,
    MAX(weight) as FattestCat
    FROM animal
    WHERE species_id = 'C';
```

SmallestCat	FattestCat
4.0	17.0

Concatenating Columns in a Group

An additional aggregate function will also allow you to summarize multiple row values in a single row by concatenating them together. This was not part of the original SQL standard and each database we are covering has implemented this differently.

MySQL and MariaDB

MySQL provides the `GROUP_CONCAT()` function that will take the data from a column and concatenate it together with commas for aggregation. You may define a custom separator, order, or only unique values with options (see the documentation).[61]

Table 127: MySQL Group_Concat Function

Function	Description
GROUP_CONCAT(expr)	Concatenate rows into a single attribute with comma separator.
GROUP_CONCAT(expr SEPARATOR expr2)	Concatenate rows into a single attribute using specified separator.

---

[61] https://dev.mysql.com/doc/refman/8.4/en/aggregate-functions.html#function_group-concat

Examples

An example would be we would like a listing of species we have available as a comma separated list.

```
SELECT GROUP_CONCAT(species_id)
    FROM species
    ORDER BY species_id;
```

GROUP_CONCAT(species_id)
C,D,H

We can `JOIN` owners to animals so that we can nicely list the owners names who own one or more living cats. Notice that the `DISTINCT` keyword was added before the expression to be aggregated. This option will concatenate a value once even if it exists in the recordset multiple times.

```
SELECT
    GROUP_CONCAT( DISTINCT
    CONCAT(first_name, ' ', last_name)
    SEPARATOR ', ')  AS Owners
    FROM animal
        JOIN owner ON owner.owner_id = animal.owner_id
    WHERE death_datetime IS NULL
    AND species_id = 'C';
```

Owners
Amy Smithson, John Clark, Susan Greene

SQLite

SQLite provides the `GROUP_CONCAT()` or `STRING_AGG()` function to perform this.[62] The `GROUP_CONCAT()` function will take an optional second argument for separator and will use a simple comma ',' if it is not included. The `STRING_AGG()` function is included for some compatibility to Microsoft's SQL Server.

Table 130: SQLite Group_Concat Function

Function	Description
GROUP_CONCAT(expr)	Concatenate rows into a single attribute with comma separator.

---

[62]https://www.sqlite.org/lang_aggfunc.html#group_concat

Function	Description
`GROUP_CONCAT( expr, separator_expr)`	Concatenate rows into a single attribute using specified separator.

Examples

We would like a comma separated list of all of the available species codes in alphabetic order.

```
SELECT GROUP_CONCAT(species_id)
    FROM species
    ORDER BY species_id;
```

GROUP_CONCAT(species_id)
C,D,H

For another example using an expression and a custom separator, we can create a single value of all the owners who currently have a balance.

```
SELECT
    GROUP_CONCAT(CONCAT(first_name,' ',last_name), ', ') AS names
    FROM owner
    JOIN ownerbalance
    ON ownerbalance.owner_id = owner.owner_id
    WHERE balance > 0;
```

names
Amy Smithson, Susan Greene

MSSQL Server

In MSSQL Server, the function to perform this operation is called `STRING_AGG()`.[63] It requires two parameters, the first is the expression to concatenate and the second is the separator to use between instances of the first.

---

[63]https://learn.microsoft.com/en-us/sql/t-sql/functions/string-agg-transact-sql?view=sql-server-ver16

Function	Description
STRING_AGG(expr, separator_expr)	Concatenate rows into a single attribute using specified separator.

Example

For a simple example, let us concatenate the gender codes together into a single column.

```
SELECT STRING_AGG(gender_id, ',')
    FROM gender;
```

(No column name)
F,M,NF,NM,U

Case

Using the Toy Store Order sample database, we have been asked a few questions.

We need to know the number of distinct items on an order and the total number of pieces that are on an order. Please show these totals for order 1407.

```
SELECT COUNT(*) AS item_count, SUM(quantity) AS piece_count
    FROM order_detail
    WHERE order_id = 1407;
```

item_count	piece_count
3	7

How many orders for part 1001 have we had from customer 101 and how many of them did they order? Also show the earliest and most recent date of an order for this part.

```
SELECT COUNT(*) AS Orders, SUM(quantity) AS TotalSales,
    MIN(order_datetime) AS FirstOrder,
    MAX(order_datetime) AS LastOrder
    FROM order_detail
    JOIN order_header
        ON order_detail.order_id = order_header.order_id
    WHERE customer_id = 101 and item_id = 1001;
```

Orders	TotalSales	FirstOrder	LastOrder
4	7	2023-01-04 10:17	2023-08-29 21:47

What was the largest order by dollar amount, the smallest, and the average order size?

```
SELECT MAX(total), MIN(total), ROUND(AVG(total),2)
    FROM order_header;
```

MAX(total)	MIN(total)	ROUND(AVG(total),2)
429.66	3.08	134.85

Exercises

For this chapter's exercises, use the Media Collection sample database.

1. How many songs do we have on our database by the band "Roach to Men" (Artist #7)? How long is the shortest, longest, and average song.

2. Return the count of tracks on the album named 'Neon Dreamscape' (Album #6) and the length of the album in minutes and seconds (total length of the tracks).

3. How much do I have invested in all of my albums? Show me the total cost of all albums, the total price of what I have sold, and the net amount I have spent on the collection I still have.

This page intentionally left blank.

Chapter 14 - SQL Grouping Data.

By grouping rows together in combination with the aggregate functions from the previous chapter, we can calculate totals, counts, averages, and other things on these groups. This is especially useful when trying to summarize transactional data for another entity or for calculating totals and sub-totals of a transaction detail.

Objectives

At the conclusion of this lesson module, students will be able to:

1. group data by one or more attributes.
2. choose which groups get returned in the recordset.
3. use aggregate functions to summarize the groups.

Grouping Data

Creating a group on different attribute values is done with the GROUP BY clause. It causes a new group to be created for each distinct value of the attribute. Grouping may be done in a complex SQL statements with JOIN and other clauses.

Table 138: Group By Clause

SQL Clause	Description
GROUP BY column...	Aggregate data by one or more specified attribute.

Examples

For example, we want to count the number of living animals by species. The WHERE clause limits the recordset before we start the grouping process. If we want to limit the groups themselves, we would use the HAVING clause which will be covered later in this chapter.

```
SELECT species_id, COUNT(*) as Living
    FROM animal
    WHERE death_datetime IS NULL
    GROUP BY species_id;
```

species_id	Living
C	6
D	1

Record Sets with Non-Aggregated Columns

Sometimes, we may want to show other columns than just the ones in our `GROUP BY` or summarised by aggregate functions. This behavior is handled differently between databases.

MySQL, MariaDB and SQLite

In the MySQL and SQLite databases, non-aggregated columns will return the first value of that column in each group. This makes writing complex statements with `GROUP BY` clauses easier, but may introduce logical errors in the results.

Examples

Suppose we want a list of owner numbers, names, and number of living animals:

```
SELECT owner.owner_id, last_name, first_name,
    COUNT(*) AS LivingAnimals
    FROM owner
    JOIN animal ON animal.owner_id = owner.owner_id
    WHERE death_datetime IS NULL
    GROUP BY owner.owner_id;
```

owner_id	last_name	first_name	LivingAnimals
1	Smithson	Amy	1
3	Greene	Susan	2
4	Luton	Lex	1
5	Clark	John	3

Because the owner name and owner_id are directly related, the `SELECT` statement is correct when it returns the first last_name and first first_name in each group.

In a second example, the statement works but the name column returns the name of the first cat and the first dog. Name is not related to the column in the `GROUP BY` clause. While this is what you asked for, it probably does not make sense and may cause errors in your understanding of the result.

```
SELECT species_id, name, SUM(weight)
    FROM animal
    GROUP BY species_id;
```

MSSQL Server

MSSQL Server does not allow columns that are not aggregated in the recordset of a `SELECT` with a `GROUP BY`. If you attempt some of the statements that work in other databases, you may receive an error like `Msg 8120, Level 16, State 1, Line xx Column 'xxx' is invalid in the select list because it` is not contained in either an aggregate function or the GROUP BY clause. To resolve this error, you will need to aggregate those un-aggregated columns. The MAX() function may be used for this.

You may do this type of aggregation in the other databases and statements will work. Many general examples in the remainder of the book will be done in this style.

Example

Suppose we want a list of owner numbers, names, and number of living animals (remembering to aggregate the last_name and first_name columns):

```
SELECT owner.owner_id, MAX(last_name), MAX(first_name),
    COUNT(*) AS LivingAnimals
    FROM owner
    JOIN animal ON animal.owner_id = owner.owner_id
    WHERE death_datetime IS NULL
    GROUP BY owner.owner_id;
```

owner_id	(No column name)	(No column name)	LivingAnimals
1	Smithson	Amy	1
3	Greene	Susan	2
4	Luton	Lex	1
5	Clark	John	3

Having

The HAVING clause, part of GROUP BY, is similar to the WHERE clause, but it acts on the results of the grouping.

Table 142: Having Clause

Function	Description
HAVING boolean_expression	Add criteria to the grouping.

Example

Generate a list of genders with count of animals but only include the groups where there are more than two in the group (exclude groups with zero, one, or two members).

```
SELECT gender_id, COUNT(*) as Animals
    FROM animal
    GROUP BY gender_id
    HAVING Animals > 2;
```

gender_id	Animals
NF	4
NM	3

Case

Using the Media Collection sample database, we have been asked a few questions.

How many songs do we have on our database for each artist, how long is the shortest, longest, and average song? Show the artist number, name, and the four values.

```
SELECT artist.artist_id, MAX(name),
    COUNT(*) AS Tracks, MAX(sec_length) AS Longest,
    MIN(sec_length) AS Shortest,
    ROUND(AVG(sec_length),0) as Average
    FROM song
    JOIN artist ON artist.artist_id = song.artist_id
    GROUP BY artist.artist_id;
```

artist_id	name	Tracks	Longest	Shortest	Average
1	Motley Grunge	15	378	94	248.0
2	Queen Ant	6	404	156	276.0
3	Roach to Men	14	345	152	286.0
4	Taylor Slow	25	409	146	267.0
5	George Wiggly	35	411	148	265.0
7	Purple Frog	25	430	140	275.0
8	Hazy Daisy	3	246	158	207.0

For all albums, show their name, the count of tracks, and the length of the album in seconds. Only show albums that have a total running time of 2000 or more seconds.

```
SELECT album.album_id, MAX(album_title),
    COUNT(*) AS Tracks, SUM(sec_length) AS Sec
    FROM album_track
    JOIN song ON song.song_id = album_track.song_id
    JOIN album ON album.album_id = album_track.album_id
    GROUP BY album.album_id
    HAVING SUM(sec_length) >= 2000;
```

album_id	album_title	Tracks	Sec
3	Can't Get More Motley	7	2002
17	Celestial Canvas	8	2041

album_id	album_title	Tracks	Sec
21	Astral Alchemy	9	2429
28	Greatest Hits	9	2322
29	Greatest Hits	7	2116

How much do I have invested in my albums by artist? Show me the artist name, cost of all albums for that artist, price of what I have sold, and the net amount I have spent on each artist.

```
SELECT artist.artist_id, MAX(name),
    COUNT(*) AS Count,
    SUM(cost) AS Cost, SUM(price) as SoldFor,
    SUM(cost)-SUM(price) AS Net
FROM album
JOIN artist ON artist.artist_id = album.artist_id
GROUP BY artist.artist_id;
```

artist_id	name	Count	Cost	SoldFor	Net
1	Motley Grunge	4	56.67	NULL	NULL
2	Queen Ant	2	23.62	NULL	NULL
3	Roach to Men	4	57.21	NULL	NULL
4	Taylor Slow	5	71.06	79.95	-8.89
5	George Wiggly	7	91.01	NULL	NULL
7	Purple Frog	7	88.53	33.5	55.03
999	Various	2	22.4	NULL	NULL

Exercises

For this chapter's exercises, use the Toy Store Order sample database.

1. We need to summarize information on order numbers 1400 to 1410. Please show the order number, date, customer number, name, number of distinct items, and total number of pieces on the order. Order output by order number.

2. How many of each part has customer 101 ordered in the past? Also show the number of orders, earliest purchase date, and most recent purchase date for each part.

This page intentionally left blank.

Chapter 15 - SQL Dates, Times, and DateTimes

Tracking and keeping temporal facts (when) is an important part of any data model, collection, or database. We humans call this time and date. While there are several common functions and keywords for handling temporal facts, each database vendor implements these functions and storage differently. This introduction will not cover all the ways to manage dates and times in the databases, but will show several basic operations with dates, times, and datetimes.

Objectives

At the conclusion of this lesson module, students will be able to:

1. read and write dates in the ISO-8601 standard date format.
2. add timezone offset information to an ISO date.
3. use an SQL function to get current datetime.
4. extract the date and time parts from a datetime value.
5. add/subtract time intervals from a datetime.
6. find the difference between two datetime values in days and seconds.
7. convert a datetime to a string for outputting in a report.

ISO-8601 Standard for Date Format

The International Standards Organization (ISO) has created thousands of standards that are used in commerce and manufacturing throughout the world. One of the standards is known as ISO-8601 and defines a standard way to write dates and times as a string value.[64] This was necessary because people in different parts of the world often write dates differently.

This section will cover much of the ISO-8601 standard but not all of it. The part covered will be implemented in SQL by most databases.

It is important to remember that the ISO-8601 date uses the **Gregorian Calendar** with twelve months and periodic leap years.[65] This is the calendar most of the world uses and has been in use since the 16th century. The ISO-8601 format also uses a 24-hour clock (without AM or PM) with 60 minutes, 60 seconds, and decimal sub-seconds.

ISO Dates

An ISO date is typically represented by a four digit year, dash '-', two-digit month, dash '-', and two digit date; like "2024-06-10", "2020-12-31", and "1776-07-04". By representing a date in this format it avoids confusion about the year, month, and date parts. It also allows for dates in ISO format to be sorted as strings.

---

[64] https://en.wikipedia.org/wiki/ISO_8601
[65] https://en.wikipedia.org/wiki/Gregorian_calendar

ISO Times

Times are expressed in a 24-hour format with a 2 digit hour, a colon ':', and a two digit minutes. Seconds may be added with another colon ':' followed by two digits and an optional decimal point and decimal fraction seconds. Times may look like '10:23', '09:07:30', '15:57', or '23:59:59.9999'.

ISO Date and Time

A datetime is created by appending a time to the end of a date separated by either a space ' ' or the capital letter 'T'. This ISO standard specifies the 'T' but most database vendors allow either. Using a space is easier to read, so that will be used in this text.

Sample ISO Date and Times:

- 2020-01-01T01:02:03
- 2024-06-18 16:58
- 2022-02-22T12:13:14.5

Time Zones

For centuries, before clocks were common, "noon" happened when the sun was at its highest in the sky. Time was based off of that moment.[66] The problem became that each and every minute of longitude would have a unique "noon" if we went strictly by the Sun. Times would be minutes different just a few miles East or West. To standardize this, we have all agreed on bands of time that follow geographic or national borders. These are called time zones.[67]

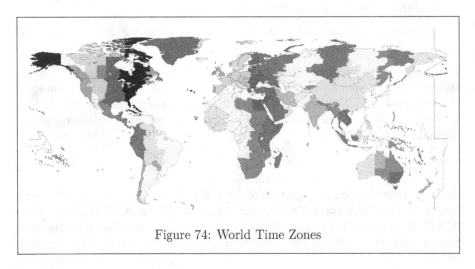

Figure 74: World Time Zones

---

[66] https://en.wikipedia.org/wiki/Noon
[67] https://en.wikipedia.org/wiki/Time_zone#/media/File:World_time_zones.svg

Time zones are expressed as the difference (less than for West and greater than for East) from the time zone known as Universal Time Coordinate (UTC) also sometimes abbreviated with the letter 'Z' and pronounced Zulu.

The international date line is exactly 12 hours ahead of and behind of UTC. This standard was first introduced in 1887. This universal basis of time was originally known as **Greenwich Mean Time** and later renamed to UTC in the 1960s with the creation of the atomic clock.[68]

Zone	Offset	Cities
China Standard Time	+08:00	Beijing
Central European Time	+01:00	Berlin, Madrid, Paris, Rome
UTC	00:00	London, Lisbon, Reykjavík
Eastern Time	-05:00	New York, Atlanta, Cincinnati, Lima, Toronto
Central Time	-06:00	Chicago, St. Louis. Houston, Mexico City
Mountain Time	-07:00	Denver, Calgary
Pacific Time	-08:00	San Francisco, Seattle, Vancouver, Tijuana
Alaska Time	-09:00	Anchorage
Hawaii Time	-10:00	Honolulu

Adding Time Zone to ISO Date and Time

An ISO-8601 date may also include time zone information. For businesses and users with more than one location or with global transactions, standardizing the expression of time and zone becomes imperative. To add a time zone to a date string, append a "+" or "-" followed by the time offset from UTC. The abbreviation "Z" may be used for UTC. Times without a timezone are assumed to be UTC.

Example ISO Dates with Time Zone:

- 2024-01-04T12:32-04:00
- 2000-12-31 17:57+01:00
- 2022-02-22T22:22.123Z

Dates in SQL

The ANSI standard defines several different functions to manipulate dates and times. Each database vendor has implemented parts of this standard, but the way dates and times are handled vary greatly. Each database will have its own section with details specific to the implementation.

---

[68]https://timemachinescorp.com/2020/12/10/the-history-of-coordinated-universal-time

MySQL and MariaDB

MySQL has column types for dates, times, and datetimes.[69] For simplicity, just the DATETIME type will be shown in detail. Additional information and functions can be found in the MySQL documentation.

Getting the Current Datetime

MySQL provides the NOW() function to return the ISO datetime.[70] You may optionally pass the function the number of digits of decimal seconds you wish to be returned.

Table 148: MySQL Now Function

Function	Description
NOW(fsp)	Return the current date and time in an ISO string. You may optionally specify how many digits of decimal precision for seconds.

Example

Show the current DATETIME to 0 and 6 decimal points of precision:

```
SELECT NOW(), NOW(6);
```

NOW()	NOW(6)
2025-01-09 13:13:27	2025-01-09 13:13:27.197432

Extracting the Date and Time Parts

If we have datetime value or expression, we can extract just the date part or the time part using either the DATE() or TIME() functions.[71] [72]

Table 150: MySQL Date and Time Functions

Function	Description
DATE(expr)	Get the date part of an expression.
TIME(expr)	Get the time part of an expression.

---

[69] https://dev.mysql.com/doc/refman/8.4/en/date-and-time-types.html

[70] https://dev.mysql.com/doc/refman/8.4/en/date-and-time-functions.html#function_now

[71] https://dev.mysql.com/doc/refman/8.4/en/date-and-time-functions.html#function_date

[72] https://dev.mysql.com/doc/refman/8.4/en/date-and-time-functions.html#function_time

Example

Get the date and time parts of the current DATETIME and from an ISO datetime:

```
SELECT DATE(NOW()), TIME(NOW()), DATE('2025-01-04 13:45:56');
```

DATE(NOW())	TIME(NOW())	DATE('2025-01-04 13:45:56')
2025-01-13	14:35:30	2025-01-04

Adding and Subtracting from DateTime Values

MySQL provides the `DATE_ADD()` and `DATE_SUB()` functions to add or subtract interval to a date, time, or datetime.[73]

Table 152: MySQL Date_Add and Date_Sub Functions

Function	Description
`DATE_ADD(datetime, interval)`	Add an interval to a date, time, or datetime.
`DATE_SUB(datetime, interval)`	Subtract an interval from a date, time, or datetime.

Intervals used in DATE_ADD and DATE_SUB start with the keyword `INTERVAL`, then a number or string part of an ISO date, followed by the length of the interval. Interval lengths include `YEAR`, `MONTH`, `DAY`, `HOUR`, `MINUTE`, and `SECOND`. Complex intervals are defined from one interval to another separated by an underscore, examples include: `YEAR_MONTH`, `DAY_MINUTE`, and `HOURS_SECOND`.

Example

Add 15 days to December 20, 2024 and add 3 days 11 hours and 55 minutes to 1:32:44 PM on January 9, 2025:

```
SELECT DATE_ADD('2024-12-20', INTERVAL 15 DAY) AS P15,
    DATE_ADD('2025-01-09 13:32:44',
    INTERVAL '3 11:55' DAY_MINUTE) AS D3H11M55;
```

P15	D3H11M55
2025-01-04	2025-01-13 01:27:44

---

[73]https://dev.mysql.com/doc/refman/8.4/en/date-and-time-functions.html#function_date-add

Difference Between Dates and Times

MySQL has several ways to calculate the number of days or seconds between two date, time, or datetime values.

Finding Difference in Days

MySQL includes the DATEDIFF() function to calculate the difference between two dates in days. Only the date part of a datetime is used in this calculation.[74]

Table 154: MySQL Datediff Function

Function	Description
DATEDIFF(expr1, expr2)	Return the difference in days.

Example

Calculate the difference, in days, from the current datetime and October 19, 2022:

```
SELECT NOW(),
    DATEDIFF(NOW(), '2022-10-19: 13:34') AS DaysAgo;
```

NOW()	DaysAgo
2025-01-31 16:57:08	835

Finding Difference in Seconds

MySQL provides the TO_SECONDS() function to return the number of seconds since year zero for a datetime. This can be used to calculate the difference between two datetimes in seconds.[75]

Table 156: MySQL To_Seconds Function

Function	Description
TO_SECONDS(expr)	Return the number of seconds since 0000-00-00 00:00:00.

Example

---

[74]https://dev.mysql.com/doc/refman/8.4/en/date-and-time-functions.html#function_datediff

[75]https://dev.mysql.com/doc/refman/8.4/en/date-and-time-functions.html#function_to-seconds

How many seconds has elapsed since midnight on 0000-00-00 to right now, how many seconds have elapsed since midnight on 0000-00-00 to 12:34:56PM on October, 19, 2022, and what is the difference from now to that date in 2022 in seconds?

```
SELECT NOW(), TO_SECONDS(NOW()) AS NowSec,
    TO_SECONDS('2022-10-19: 12:34:56') As SecOn19Th,
    TO_SECONDS(NOW()) - TO_SECONDS('2022-10-19: 12:34:56')
    AS SecondsAgo;
```

NOW()	NowSec	SecOn19Th	SecondsAgo
2025-01-31 16:59:05	63905561945	63833356800	72205145

Output Formatting of DateTime Values

The `DATE_FORMAT` function is a very powerful way to extract parts of a time, date, or datetime and return a string.[76] It loosely follows the 'C' language 'strftime()' function but the arguments are reversed and the format string has some differences.

Table 158: MySQL Date_Format Function

Function	Description
`DATE_FORMAT(expr, format_string)`	Format a date based on formatting string.

In the format string, percent signs '%' followed by a letter are replaced with parts of the date. Other letters, symbols, and spaces will be retained in the returned string. The list below shows some of the formatting options available. Please see the MySQL documentation for a full list.

- Year, Month and Day
    - %Y - Year, numeric, four digits
    - %y - Year, numeric (two digits)
    - %m - Month, numeric (00..12)
    - %c - Month, numeric (0..12)
    - %d - Day of the month, numeric (00..31)
    - %e - Day of the month, numeric (0..31)
- Hours, Minutes, and Seconds
    - %H - Hour (00..23)
    - %k - Hour (0..23)
    - %h - Hour (01..12)

---

[76]https://dev.mysql.com/doc/refman/8.4/en/date-and-time-functions.html#function_date-format

141

- **%l** - Hour (1..12)
- **%i** - Minutes, numeric (00..59)
- **%S** - Seconds (00..59)
- Selected Other
  - **%M** - Month name (January..December)
  - **%b** - Abbreviated month name (Jan..Dec)
  - **%W** - Weekday name (Sunday..Saturday)
  - **%a** - Abbreviated weekday name (Sun..Sat)
  - **%w** - Day of the week (0=Sunday..6=Saturday)
  - **%j** - Day of year (001..366)
  - **%p** - AM or PM
  - **%%** - A literal % character

Example

Reformat an ISO date and time into the more common US date and time as MM-DD-YYYY HH:MM AM/PM followed by the day number in the year:

```
SELECT DATE_FORMAT('2025-02-14 13:34', '%m/%d/%Y %l:%i %p (%j)')
    AS DateAndDay;
```

Format explained:

```
%m/%d/%Y %l:%i %p (%j)
^^  .   .   .    .   .      2 digit month
 ^. .   .   .    .   .      /
  ^^ .   .   .    .   .     2 digit day of month
   ^. .   .    .   .        /
    ^^  .   .    .   .      4 digit year
      ^.   .    .   .       space
      ^^   .    .   .       hour (1-12)
        ^.    .    .        :
        ^    .    .         minute
          ^.    .           space
          ^^    .           AM or PM
            ^^.             space and open parenthesis
            ^^              day of the year
             ^             close parenthesis
```

DateAndDay
02/14/2025 1:34 PM (045)

SQLite

SQLite does not have built in column types to store dates, times, or datetimes. They are stored in one of 3 ways: [77] [78]

1. as an ISO Date and Time string;
2. as a decimal Julian day number (days since 12:00 PM on January 1, 4713 BC); or
3. as an integer UNIX timestamp (number of seconds since 1970-01-01T00:00:00Z).

One should be careful storing dates using a UNIX timestamp, because the current maximum value of a signed 32-bit integer causes the date to reach an overflow on 2038-01-19. Usually, storing dates in ISO format in a text field is the preferred method for storing date and time values in SQLite.

DateTime Values

Because SQLite does not have a specific data type for dates, times, or datetimes, a string becomes a valid date, time, or datetime if it is in the ISO format. SQLite provides three functions (`DATETIME()`, `DATE()`, and `TIME()`) that will accept a time value (see list below) and will return either a date, time, or datetime as a string.

Table 160: SQLite DateTime Function

Function	Description
DATETIME(time_value, modifiers...)	Return the complete date and time string of the time_value passed (adjusted by the modifiers).

Formats of date and time values used in SQLite date functions: [79]

1. 'YYYY-MM-DD' - Date with no time (00:00:00 assumed)
2. 'YYYY-MM-DD HH:MM' or 'YYYY-MM-DDTHH:MM' - Date with Hours and Minutes
3. 'YYYY-MM-DD HH:MM:SS' or 'YYYY-MM-DDTHH:MM:SS' - Date with Hours, Minutes, and Seconds
4. 'YYYY-MM-DD HH:MM:SS.SSS' or 'YYYY-MM-DDTHH:MM:SS.SSS' Date with Hours, Minutes, Seconds and Fractional Seconds
5. 'HH:MM', 'HH:MM:SS', or 'HH:MM:SS.SSS' - Time values without date (2000-01-01 is assumed)
6. 'now' - The current system date and time.
7. '#######' or '#######.#####'- Julian day number with fractional days or unix timestamp (you should use the modifier 'julianday' or 'unixepoch' to differentiate).

---

[77] https://en.wikipedia.org/wiki/Julian_day
[78] https://en.wikipedia.org/wiki/Unix_time
[79] https://www.sqlite.org/lang_datefunc.html#tmval

Getting the current DATETIME

Use the 'now' time string to return the current datetime in the `DATETIME()` function.

Example

```
SELECT DATETIME('now');
```

DATETIME('now')
2025-01-09 18:00:44

Using Modifiers on DATETIMEs

You may also use the modifiers on the `DATETIME` function to add intervals, subtract intervals, find the first day of the month, first day of the year, or even the next weekday. Below is a list of selected modifiers. Please refer to the documentation for a full list of available.[80]

- Add or Subtract Time and Date Intervals
  - 'NNN days', 'NNN hours', 'NNN minutes', 'NNN seconds', 'NNN months', or 'NNN years' - Add or subtract a specific period.
  - '±HH:MM', '±HH:MM:SS', or '±HH:MM:SS.SSS' - Add or subtract a length of time.
  - '±YYYY-MM-DD' - Add or subtract a number of years, months, and days.
  - '±YYYY-MM-DD HH:MM', '±YYYY-MM-DD HH:MM:SS', or '±YYYY-MM-DD HH:MM:SS.SSS' - Add or subtract years, months, days, and time.
- Start of
  - 'start of month', or 'start of year' - go back to the first day of the month or year.
  - 'start of day' - go back to midnight.
- Next
  - 'weekday N' - Advance if needed to the next weekday where Sunday = 0, Monday = 1...

Example

As an example we want to add three days to a date, find the first of the month from a specific date, or find the second Tuesday of a month.

```
SELECT DATETIME('2024-05-06 12:03','+0000-00-03') AS Plus3,
    DATETIME('2024-05-06 12:03','start of month') AS Start,
    DATETIME('2025-10-01','weekday 2','weekday 2')
        AS SecondTue;
```

---

[80]https://www.sqlite.org/lang_datefunc.html#dtmods

Plus3	Start	SecondTue
2024-05-09 12:03:00	2024-05-01 00:00:00	2025-10-07 00:00:00

Extracting the Date and Time Parts

If we have datetime or a time value in SQLite, we can easily extract just the date part or the time part using either the `DATE()` or `TIME()` functions.

Table 163: SQLite Date and Time functions

Function	Description
`DATE(time_value, modifiers...)`	Get the date part of the time_value passed (adjusted by the modifiers).
`TIME(time_value, modifiers...)`	Get the time part of the time_value passed (adjusted by the modifiers).

Example

Show the date part and time part of right now. Also show the date part of an ISO datetime value:

```
SELECT DATE('now'), TIME('now'), DATE('2025-01-04 13:45:56');
```

DATE('now')	TIME('now')	DATE('2025-01-04 13:45:56')
2025-01-13	19:28:34	2025-01-04

Difference Between Dates and Times

SQLite provides three ways to find the difference between two time values: 1) returning an ISO string representing the difference, 2) returning the duration in decimal days, or 3) returning the difference in seconds.

Difference as ISO Date

The `TIMEDIFF()` fuction will take to ISO datetimes and calculate the difference betweene them. A datetime interval in ISO format will be returned.

Table 165: SQLite Timediff Function

Function	Description
`TIMEDIFF(time_value, time_value)`	Return a human-readable (ISO format) time difference from two time values.

Example

In this example, we subtract two dates to get the length of time between them. Durations returned by `TIMEDIFF()` may be used directly as time modifiers in the `DATETIME()`, `DATE()`, and `TIME()` functions.

```
SELECT TIMEDIFF('2025-02-14 13:34', '2000-09-06 06:00')
    AS TimeSince,
    DATETIME('2000-09-06 06:00',
        TIMEDIFF('2025-02-14 13:34', '2000-09-06 06:00'))
        AS AddedBack;
```

TimeSince	AddedBack
+0024-05-08 07:34:00.000	2025-02-14 13:34:00

Getting Julian Days and the Difference in Days

We can easily find the decimal number of days since 12:00 PM on January 1, 4713 BC, by using the `JULIANDAY()` function. By subtracting the Julian day number of two different time values we can find the difference in days.[81]

Table 167: SQLite Julianday Function

Function	Description
`JULIANDAY(time_value, modifiers...)`	Calculate the Julian day for the time value.

Examples

Find the difference in decimal days from the moment when we were married (11AM on October 11, 2008) to the start of our lunch date at 1:30PM on Valentines day of 2025:

```
SELECT JULIANDAY('2025-02-14 13:30') AS ValentinesLunch,
    JULIANDAY('2008-10-11 11:00') AS MarriedOn,
    JULIANDAY('2025-02-14 13:30') -
        JULIANDAY('2008-10-11 11:00') AS DaysMarried;
```

ValentinesLunch	MarriedOn	DaysMarried
2460721.0625	2454750.95833333	5970.10416666651

Another example of difference; let's calculate the age of each animal at their death.

---

[81]https://www.sqlite.org/lang_datefunc.html#jlndy

```
SELECT animal_id, name,
    ROUND((JULIANDAY(death_datetime) - JULIANDAY(birth_datetime))
        / 365.25, 1) AS AgeAtDeath
    FROM animal
    WHERE death_datetime;
```

animal_id	name	AgeAtDeath
2	Bobo	13.8
4	Bonnie	4.6

Getting Unix Timestamp and the Difference in Seconds

The UNIX clock started on 1970-01-01T00:00:00Z and the timestamp value has been updated for every second since. The `UNIXEPOCH()` function returns the number of seconds since the epoch began. If we want the time difference in seconds, we could easily calculate the timestamp for the two time values and subtract.[82]

Table 170: SQLite Unixepoch Function

Function	Description
UNIXEPOCH(time_value, modifiers...)	Calculate the UNIX timestamp value for the time value.

Example

Calculate the UNIX timestamp value, in seconds, for two ISO dates. Also show the difference: in seconds calculated two different ways:

```
SELECT UNIXEPOCH('2025-02-14 13:34'),
    UNIXEPOCH('2000-09-06 06:00'),
    UNIXEPOCH('2025-02-14 13:34') -
        UNIXEPOCH('2000-09-06 06:00') AS Seconds,
    ( JULIANDAY('2025-02-14 13:34') -
        JULIANDAY('2000-09-06 06:00') ) * 24 * 60 * 60
        AS JulianSeconds;
```

UNIXEPOCH('2025-02-14 13:34')	UNIXEPOCH('2000-09-06 06:00')	Seconds	JulianSeconds
1739540040	968220000	771320040	771320039.999986

---

[82]https://www.sqlite.org/lang_datefunc.html#uepch

Output Formatting of DateTime Values

On many systems, there is a function in the standard C library called `strftime()`.[83] It will take a UNIX timestamp and build a string for display and storage based on a format string. SQLite implements a similar function also called `STRFTIME()`.[84]

Table 172: SQLite Strftime Function

Function	Description
`STRFTIME(format_string, time_value)`	Returns a time value formatted based on the format string.

In the format string, percent signs '%' followed by a letter are replaced with parts of the date. Other letters, symbols, and spaces will be retained in the returned string. The list below shows some of the formatting options available. Please see the SQLite documentation for a full list.

- ISO 1860 Date Parts
  - `%F` - ISO date `YYYY-MM-DD`
  - `%R` - ISO time `HH:MM`
  - `%T` - ISO time with seconds `HH:MM:SS`
- Year, Month and Day
  - `%Y` - four digit year `0000-9999`
  - `%m` - two digit month `01-12`
  - `%d` - two digit day of month `01-31`
  - `%e` - day of month without leading zero `1-31`
- Hours, Minutes, and Seconds
  - `%H` - two digit hour `00-24`
  - `%I` - two digit hour for 12-hour clock `01-12`
  - `%k` - hour without leading zero `0-24`
  - `%l` - hour without leading zero for 12-hour clock `1-12`
  - `%M` - two digit minute `00-59`
  - `%S` - two digit seconds `00-59`
  - `%f` - two digit with fractional seconds `SS.SSS`
- Selected Other
  - `%p` - `AM` or `PM`
  - `%P` - `am` or `pm`
  - `%j` - day of year `001-366`
  - `%U` - week of year - week 01 starts on the first Sunday `00-53`
  - `%w` - day of week starting on Sunday `0-6`
  - `%%` - `%`

---

[83] https://pubs.opengroup.org/onlinepubs/009696799/functions/strftime.html
[84] https://www.sqlite.org/lang_datefunc.html#strftm

Example

Reformat an ISO date and time into the more common US date and time as MM-DD-YY HH:MM AM/PM followed by the day number in the year:

```
SELECT STRFTIME('%m/%d/%g %I:%M %p (%j)', '2025-02-14 13:34')
    AS DateAndDay;
```

Format explained:

```
%m/%d/%g %I:%M %p (%j)
^^ .  .  .   .   .   .      2 digit month
  ^ .  .  .   .   .   .      /
   ^^ .  .   .   .   .      2 digit day of month
     ^ .  .   .   .   .      /
      ^^ .   .   .   .      2 digit year
        ^ .   .   .   .      space
         ^^ .   .   .      hour (1-12)
           ^ .   .   .      :
            ^ .   .      minute
             ^.   .      space
              ^^ .      AM or PM
               ^^.      space and open parenthesis
                ^^      day of the year
                 ^      close parenthesis
```

DateAndDay
02/14/25 01:34 PM (045)

MSSQL Server

Microsoft's MSSQL Server has a complete suite of types and functions to handle date, time, and datetime values. As with the other database engines, MSSQL is unique in how time is handled.

Getting the Current Datetime

To get the current datetime from the database, in Microsoft's MSSQL Server, we will use the GETDATE() function.[85]

Table 174: MSSQL Getdate() Function

Function	Description
GETDATE()	Return the current datetime value.

---

[85]https://learn.microsoft.com/en-us/sql/t-sql/functions/getdate-transact-sql?view=sql-server-ver16

Example

Get the current date and time from the server:

```
SELECT GETDATE();
```

(No column name)
2025-01-05 08:28:22.837

Extracting the Date and Time Parts

MSSQL Server does not have simple functions to extract the date and time portions from a datetime value. To accomplish this, we will use the `CAST()` function that will change a value from one type to another.[86]

Table 176: MSSQL Casting Datetime Values to Date and Time

Function	Description
`CAST(expr AS DATE)`	Convert a value to a date, removing non-date part.
`CAST(expr AS TIME)`	Convert a value to a time, removing non-time part.

Example

This example will display the current datetime and split out the date and tima parts:

```
SELECT GETDATE(),
    CAST(GETDATE() AS DATE),
    CAST (GETDATE() AS TIME);
```

(No column name)	(No column name)	(No column name)
2025-01-13 22:18:59.697	2025-01-13	22:18:59.697002

Adding and Subtracting from DateTime Values

The `DATEADD()` function will add integer intervals to a date. Use a negative value for the interval if you wish to subtract from a date or time.[87] The number argument must be an integer value and any decimal fraction will be ignored in the calculation.

---

[86] https://learn.microsoft.com/en-us/sql/t-sql/functions/cast-and-convert-transact-sql?view=sql-server-ver16

[87] https://learn.microsoft.com/en-us/sql/t-sql/functions/dateadd-transact-sql?view=sql-server-ver16

Table 178: MSSQL Dateadd Function

Function	Description
`DATEADD(date_part, number, date)`	Add integer number to part of a date.

The following table shows selected date parts used in the function. Please see the documentation for all options and additional examples.

date_part	description
`YEAR`	add full years
`QUARTER`	add quarter (3 months)
`MONTH`	add months
`DAY`	add days
`WEEK`	add full weeks (7 days)
`HOUR`	add hours
`MINUTE`	add minutes
`SECOND`	add seconds
`MILLISECOND`	add one thousandth (1/1000) of second
`MICROSECOND`	add one millionth (1/1000000) of second
`NANOSECOND`	add one billionth (1/1000000000) of a second

Example

Add three months to 9:34:56 AM on January 14, 2025 and then subtract 12 hours from the same moment in time:

```
SELECT DATEADD(month, 3, '2025-01-14 09:34:56') AS Plus3Day,
    DATEADD(hour, -12, '2025-01-14 09:34:56') AS Less12Hour;
```

Plus3Day	Less12Hour
2025-04-14 09:34:56.000	2025-01-13 21:34:56.000

Difference Between Dates and Times

MSSQL has a function called `DATEDIFF()` that will calculate the difference between two dates in a variety of units.[88] The date parts used in this function are listed above in the `DATEADD()` function.

---

[88]https://learn.microsoft.com/en-us/sql/t-sql/functions/datediff-transact-sql?view=sql-server-ver16

Function	Description
`DATEDIFF(date_part, start_date, end_date)`	Returns the integer difference from start to end in date_part units.

Examples

Calculate the difference in years, days, and seconds between several date and time values.

```
SELECT DATEDIFF(YEAR, '1776-07-04', '2025-01-14 10:05:58')
    AS USAge,
    DATEDIFF(DAY, '1776-07-04', '2025-01-14 10:05:58')
    AS USAgeDay,
    DATEDIFF(SECOND, '2025-01-14 03:45:23', '2025-01-14 10:05:58')
    AS Seconds;
```

USAge	USAgeDay	Seconds
249	90774	22835

Using the Vet Office database, What is the average age in months of living animals by species?

```
SELECT animal.species_id,
    MAX(description) AS Description,
    COUNT(*) as Aimals,
    AVG(DATEDIFF(month, birth_datetime, GETDATE())) AS AgeInMon
    FROM animal
    JOIN species ON animal.species_id = species.species_id
    WHERE death_datetime IS NULL
    GROUP BY animal.species_id
```

species_id	Description	Aimals	AgeInMon
C	Feline	6	56
D	Canine	1	50

Output Formatting of DateTime Values

To convert a date, time, or datetime to a string for output, we will use the `CONVERT()` function in MSSQL with the result type of `NVARCHAR` and a format number.[89]

---

[89]https://learn.microsoft.com/en-us/sql/t-sql/functions/cast-and-convert-transact-sql?view=sql-server-ver16

Table 184: MSSQL Convert Function to Format Dates

Function	Description
`CONVERT(NVARCHAR, date, format_number)`	Return date, time, or datetime as a string in the specified format.

The following table includes many common date conversion codes. For a complete list of format codes, see the documentation for the **CONVERT()** function.

Table 185: Selected Formats for Date to String Casting

format_number	format	format_number with century	format	description
		0 or 100	mon dd yyyy hh:miAM (or PM)	Default for datetime
1	mm/dd/yy	101	mm/dd/yyyy	U.S.
2	yy.mm.dd	102	yyyy.mm.dd	ANSI
3	dd/mm/yy	103	dd/mm/yyyy	British/French
4	dd.mm.yy	104	dd.mm.yyyy	German
		9 or 109	mon dd yyyy hh:mi:ss:mmmAM (or PM)	Default + milliseconds
11	yy/mm/dd	111	yyyy/mm/dd	JAPAN
		20 or 120	yyyy-mm-dd hh:mi:ss (24-hour)	ODBC canonical
		21, 25, or 121	yyyy-mm-dd hh:mi:ss.mmm (24-hour)	ODBC canonical (with milliseconds)
		23	yyyy-mm-dd	ISO8601
		126	yyyy-mm-ddThh:mi:ss.mmm	ISO8601 (no spaces)

Example

Convert the current datetime into several different formats.

```
SELECT CONVERT(NVARCHAR, GETDATE() ,0) as DFLT,
    CONVERT(NVARCHAR, GETDATE() ,101) as US,
    CONVERT(NVARCHAR, GETDATE() ,103) as UK_FR,
    CONVERT(NVARCHAR, GETDATE() ,21) as ISO_space;
```

DFLT	US	UK_FR	ISO_space
Jan 14 2025 8:00PM	01/14/2025	14/01/2025	2025-01-14 20:00:58.187

Case

Using the Toy Store Order sample database, we have been asked a few questions.

We are interested in our Christmas toy sales and would like a report of each item with total sole for the period of November and December 2023.

```
SELECT item.item_id, MAX(item.description),
    SUM(order_detail.quantity)
    FROM order_header
    JOIN order_detail
    ON order_header.order_id = order_detail.order_id
```

```
JOIN item ON order_detail.item_id = item.item_id
WHERE order_datetime >= '2023-11-01'
AND order_datetime <= '2023-12-31'
GROUP BY item.item_id
;
```

item_id	description	sum(order_detail.quantity)
1001	Blue Flying Disk	56
1002	Red Flying Disk	38
1003	Rainbow Flying Disk	72
1010	Yellow Butterfly Yo-Yo	49
1011	Blue Royal Yo-Yo	49
1012	Giant Wooden Yo-Yo	56
1018	Pack of Yo-Yo Strings	59
1019	Yo-Yo Wax	29
1020	Cards Against Data	45
1022	Game of Life Improvement	56
1023	Never Ending Bord Game	34
1024	Clueless Risk	61

What customers purchased something in the first quarter of 2024 having 2 or more orders.

```
SELECT customer.customer_id, MAX(name), COUNT(*) AS Orders,
    SUM(total) as TotalOfOrders
    FROM order_header
    JOIN customer
    ON order_header.customer_id = customer.customer_id
    WHERE order_datetime >= '2024-01-01'
    AND order_datetime < '2024-04-01'
    GROUP BY customer.customer_id
    HAVING COUNT(*) >= 2;
```

customer_id	name	Orders	TotalOfOrders
33	Yolanda Miranda	2	170.95
40	Javier Wells	2	418.02
46	Christopher Bradford	2	121.87
50	David Bonilla	2	269.73
56	Jeffrey Steele	2	171.64
59	Alejandro Edwards	2	215.79

Exercises

Use the Media Collection database to answer these questions:

1. What is the average age (how long have we owned it in years to one decimal place) for albums we still own.
2. Show all albums we have sold listing their id, title, date sold, price sold, profit, years we owned it, and a calculated simple interest return on our investment. Simple interest can be calculated with $R = (A - P) / (P * T)$ where R is the interest rate, A is the final value, P is the principle (original investment), and T is the time in years.

This page intentionally left blank.

Chapter 16 - SQL A Few String Functions

You have seen strings in your select results. They are sequences of letters, numbers, and symbols stored in columns. You may not perform arithmetic on them, but there are several functions that allow you to modify and to slice them into individual letters or parts.

Objectives

At the conclusion of this lesson module, students will be able to:

1. concatenate (join) strings together with or without adding a separator or whiter space.
2. change a string to all upper case or all lower case.
3. remove white space (spaces, tabs, and other characters) from the beginning, ending, or from both ends of a string.
4. calculate the length of a string.
5. extract a substring from a larger string.
6. be able to format a number to a string in the current locale.

Concatenating Strings

The word **concatenate** was defined in a previous chapter but means to link or join together. In the context of a string, concatenate means to append one string on to the end of another thus creating a new string. This section introduces the `CONCAT()` function.

Table 189: Function to Concatenate String

Function	Description
CONCAT(string, string...)	Join strings one after the other into a longer string.

The `CONCAT` function may accept 2 or more arguments and will keep appending the strings together to return a single string.

Example

Concatenate the letters 'a' and 'b' then concatenate the author's first name a space and their last name:

```
SELECT CONCAT('a','b'), CONCAT('James',' ','Reneau');
```

CONCAT('a','b')	CONCAT('James',' ','Reneau')
ab	James Reneau

157

Concatenate Operators

In specific database implementations, there may be shortcuts that will perform concatenation for you. The standard way is to use the CONCAT() function, but you may see these alternatives.

SQLite

You may use the CONCAT() function or the || operator to concatenate strings.[90]

Table 191: SQLite Concatenate Operator

Operator	Description
expr1 || expr2	Concatenate expr2 to the end of expr1

Example

Use the SQLite concatenate operator to join three strings together:

```
SELECT 'this' || ' and ' || 'that';
```

'this'	' and '
this and that	

MSSQL Server

the CONCAT() function or the + (addition) operator to concatenate strings.[91]

Table 193: MSSQL Concatenate Operator

Operator	Description
expr1 + expr2	The addition operator will perform concatenation if both expressions are strings

Example

Use the MSSQL addition operator to concatenate three strings together:

```
SELECT 'this' + ' and ' + 'that';
```

---

[90]https://www.sqlite.org/lang_expr.html

[91]https://learn.microsoft.com/en-us/sql/t-sql/language-elements/string-concatenation-transact-sql?view=sql-server-ver16

(No column name)
this and that

Concatenating Strings with A Delimiter

In most database variants, the `CONCAT_WS()` function performs concatenation and add a delimiter between the elements being concatenated. In many cases this delimiter is a single space, but any string may be used as a delimiter.

Table 195: Function to Concatenate Strings with a Delimiter

Function	Description
`CONCAT_WS(delimiter, string, string...)`	Concatenate strings with a delimiter between them.

Example

Concatenate three words together with a blank between them and concatenate four numbers with a space and a comma separating them:

```
SELECT CONCAT_WS(',','this','and','that') AS Comma,
    CONCAT_WS(', ', 234, 678, 2356, 8976) AS SpComma;
```

Comma	SpComma
this,and,that	234, 678, 2356, 8976

Changing Case

Another group of common string functions are the `UPPER()` and `LOWER()` functions. They do what their names say and turn the characters in a string to all upper or all lower case.

Table 197: Case Changing Functions

Function	Description
`UPPER( string )`	Change all the letters in a string to upper case.
`LOWER( string )`	Change all the letters in a string to lower case.

Example

Turn the two strings to all upper case letters and all lower case letters:

```
SELECT UPPER('HoW nOw'), LOWER('BrOwN CoW.');
```

159

UPPER('HoW nOw')	LOWER('BrOwN CoW.')
HOW NOW	brown cow.

Trimming White-space

The TRIM(), LTRIM(), and RTRIM() functions take a string and remove white-space from the ends of the string. Use these functions to clean up extra spaces, tabs, return, and other characters that users may inadvertently type in.

Table 199: Functions to Remove Whitespace

Function	Description
LTRIM(string)	Strip white space (spaces, tabs, returns, and others) from the left side string.
RTRIM(string)	Strip white space (spaces, tabs, returns, and others) from the right side of a string.
TRIM(string)	Strip white space (spaces, tabs, returns, and others) from both ends of a string.

Example

In this example, we will trim left, right, and both off of a string with blanks on both ends. A colon will be added to the start and end of the string after the trim so that the whitespace is visible in the output.

```
SELECT CONCAT(':', LTRIM('  word  '), ':') AS LeftTrim,
    CONCAT(':', RTRIM('  word  '), ':') AS RightTrim,
    CONCAT(':', TRIM('  word  '), ':') AS BothTrim;
```

LeftTrim	RightTrim	BothTrim
:word · · :	: · · word:	:word:

String Length

Often times we need to know the length of a string and not the actual string itself. Each database has a function to return the length in characters, they are shown in the table below.[92] [93] [94]

---

[92]https://dev.mysql.com/doc/refman/8.4/en/string-functions.html#function_length

[93]https://learn.microsoft.com/en-us/sql/t-sql/functions/len-transact-sql?view=sql-server-ver16

[94]https://www.sqlite.org/lang_corefunc.html#length

Function	Description	SQLite	MySQL	MSSQL
LEN(expr)	Returns the length of a string in number of characters or symbols.			Yes
LENGTH(expr)	Returns the length of a string in number of characters or symbols.	Yes	Yes	

Example - MySQL and SQLite

Return the length of the two strings.

```
SELECT LENGTH('Name'), LENGTH('abcdefghijklmnopqrstuvwxyz');
```

LENGTH('Name')	LENGTH('abcdefghijklmnopqrstuvwxyz')
4	26

Example - MSSql Server

Return the length of the two strings.

```
SELECT LEN(12345), LEN('Now is the time for all good...');
```

(No column name)	(No column name)
5	31

Slicing a String into Smaller Pieces

We often need to extract characters from either end or the middle of a string. For example, we need to get the first initial or the third character of a part number. SQL has several functions to do these types of operations.

Getting a General Substring

All SQL dialects give a function to extract part of a string. There are slight variances in the arguments, and they are described below.[95] [96] [97]

Table 204: Substring Functions

Function	Description	SQLite	MySQL	MSSQL
SUBSTR(expr, start)	Returns from start to end of string	Yes	Yes	
SUBSTR(expr, start, len)	Returns len characters from start position	Yes	Yes	
SUBSTRING(expr, start)	Returns from start to end of string	Yes	Yes	
SUBSTRING(expr, start, len)	Returns len characters from start position	Yes	Yes	Yes

---

[95] https://www.sqlite.org/lang_corefunc.html#substr

[96] https://dev.mysql.com/doc/refman/8.4/en/string-functions.html#function_substr

[97] https://learn.microsoft.com/en-us/sql/t-sql/functions/substring-transact-sql?view=sql-server-ver16

The first letter is 1 and starts counting with the left side. If length parameter is omitted, then the sub-string to the end will be returned.

In SQLite and MySQL, indexes may also be a negative number and starts from the right side of the string.

Example

For example, we would like to extract the 12th through 16th letter from the alphabet, and the 20th to the end.

```
SELECT
    SUBSTRING('abcdefghijklmnopqrstuvwxyz', 12, 5)
    AS Letter12,
    SUBSTRING('abcdefghijklmnopqrstuvwxyz', 20, 99999)
    AS string20toend;
```

Letter12	string20toend
lmnop	tuvwxyz

Getting the Right or Left Side

MySQL, MariaDB, and MSSQL Server

The `RIGHT()` and `LEFT()` functions are a shortcut for `SUBSTR()` and will slice a sub-string off of the right or left ends of a string up to the specified length.[98]

Table 206: Right and Left Functions

Function	Description
`RIGHT(expr, length)`	Return up to length characters from the right end of a string.
`LEFT(expr, length)`	Return up to length characters from the left end of a string.

Example

For example, in the waiting room we want to display owner's initials so that they would be able to recognize themselves, but in a way that still maintains their privacy.

```
SELECT owner_id,
    CONCAT( LEFT(first_name,1), LEFT(last_name,1) ) AS Initials
    FROM owner;
```

---

[98] https://learn.microsoft.com/en-us/sql/t-sql/functions/left-transact-sql?view=sql-server-ver16

owner_id	Initials
1	AS
2	HR
3	SG
4	LL
5	JC

SQLite

SQLite does not support the `RIGHT()` and `LEFT()` functions, but there are simple substitutions using the `SUBSTR()` function.

Table 208: Right and Left Alternatives for SQLite

Function	Description
SUBSTR(expr, -len)	Use a negative length to start from the right end of the string.
SUBSTR(expr, 1, len)	Use the starting position of one and limit the length to extract from the left side.

Example

For example in the waiting room, we want to display owner's partial phone number so that they would be able to recognize themselves, but in a way that still maintains their privacy. We want to show the first 3 digits, the last 3 digits and the 7th digit with periods and dashes.

```
SELECT owner_id,
    CONCAT(
        SUBSTR(phone, 1, 4), '.-',SUBSTR(phone,7,1),
        '..-.', SUBSTR(phone, -3) ) AS Phone
    FROM owner;
```

owner_id	Phone
1	1-55.-5..-.467
2	1-55.-5..-.712
3	1-55.-5..-.543
4	1-55.-5..-.988
5	1-55.-5..-.111

Formatting Numbers

The details of how to format numbers into the desires format differs between the various databases. We will cover number formatting in each one separately.

MySQL and MariaDB

MySQL does not have a single formatting function like some databases. Each formatting operation is handled by a different function.

Formatting a Decimal Number

The `FORMAT()` function is used to return a pretty string with separators and a fixed number of decimal places.[99]

Table 210: MYSQL Format Function

Function	Description
`FORMAT(number, decimal_places)`	Format a number in the current locale's standard format.

Example

Format two decimal lumbers to 2 and 4 decimal points:

```
SELECT FORMAT(1234567.8, 2), FORMAT(10.12345, 4);
```

FORMAT(1234567.8, 2)	FORMAT(10.12345, 4)
1,234,567.80	10.1235

Padding Right, Left, and Zero Fill

MySQL provides two functions `RPAD()` and `LPAD()` that will right or left justify a string or number in a field of spaces or a specified character.[100] [101]

Table 212: MYSQL Padding a String Functions

Function	Description
`LPAD(expr, length)`	Left justify expression in spaces to length.
`LPAD(expr, length, fill)`	Left justify expression in fill character to length.
`RPAD(expr, length)`	Right justify expression in spaces to length.
`RPAD(expr, length, fill)`	Right justify expression in fill character to length.

---

[99] https://dev.mysql.com/doc/refman/8.4/en/string-functions.html#function_format
[100] https://dev.mysql.com/doc/refman/8.4/en/string-functions.html#function_lpad
[101] https://dev.mysql.com/doc/refman/8.4/en/string-functions.html#function_rpad

Example

Right justify the string 'foo' into a 10 space field (concatenate 'Z' on both ends to show the spaces), right justify the number 99 in a zero fill of 7, and left justify the string 'bar' in a field of 10 spaces (concatenate 'X" on both ends):

```
select CONCAT('Z', LPAD('foo', 10), 'Z') AS spLeft,
    LPAD(99, 7, '0') AS 0Left,
    CONCAT('X', RPAD('bar', 10), 'X') AS spRight;
```

spLeft	0Left	spRight
Z · · · · · · · fooZ	0000099	Xbar · · · · · · · X

SQLite

Format Numbers and Strings

In SQLite, we use the **FORMAT()** function for converting numbers to strings and creating pleasing output.[102] It works like the **printf()** function found in the 'C' language and the **STRFTIME()** function for formatting dates and times.

Table 214: SQLITE Format Function

Function	Description
FORMAT(format_string, expression...)	Use format string to build zero or more expressions into a string.

Percent signs '%' followed by a letter and other characters, in the format string, are replaced with expressions passed to the function. Other letters, symbols, and spaces will be retained in the returned string. The list below shows some of the formatting options available. Please see the SQLite documentation for a full list.[103]

- Integers
    - %d or %i - Signed integer
    - %u - Unsigned integer
    - %x or %X - Hexadecimal number (base 16)
    - %o - Octal number (base 8)
- Decimal
    - %f - Decimal
    - %e or '%E' - Exponential notation
    - %g or %G - Decimal or exponential notation
- String

---

[102] https://www.sqlite.org/lang_corefunc.html#format
[103] https://www.sqlite.org/printf.html

- **%s** - Expression as a string
- **%Q** - SQL safe quoted string.
- Selected Other
  - **%%** - A literal % character

Example

Create a format string that will display an integer, a string and a string in parenthesis. Show all living animals and their id, name, and species using the format:

```
SELECT FORMAT('%i %s (%s)', animal_id, name, species_id)
    AS AnimalInfo FROM animal
    WHERE death_datetime IS NULL;
```

Format explained:

```
%i %s (%s)
^^  .   .        integer
  ^.    .        space
  ^^    .        string
    ^^.          space and an open parenthesis
      ^^         string
       ^         close parenthesis
```

AnimalInfo
1 Kitty (C)
3 Daisy (C)
5 Cookie (C)
6 Cookie (D)
7 Penny (C)
8 Holly (C)
9 Rosie (C)

Optional Width in Formatting

You may add an optional width between the % and the format letter. If the width expression is a positive number, then the justification will be right to that width. A negative length will cause justification to the left. Integers may be zero filled by adding a zero before the length.

Example

The following example can be a bit confusing. Each part of the format strings will be explained after the output:

```
SELECT FORMAT('X%-6sX%3sX','aa','bb') AS StrLens,
    FORMAT('Z%6iZ%-5iZ%07iZ', 1, 2, 3) as IntLens;
```

Format explained:

```
X%-6sX%3sX
^.    .         X
 ^^^^ .         left justify a string in 6 spaces
    ^.          X
     ^^^         right justify a string in 3 spaces
        ^        X
```

and

```
Z%6iZ%-5iZ%07iZ
^.   .     .     Z
 ^^^ .     .     right justify an integer in 6 spaces
    ^.     .     Z
     ^^^^  .     left justify an integer in 5 spaces
        ^.       Z
         ^^^^    right justify an integer in 7 zeros
            ^ Z
```

StrLens	IntLens
Xaa · · · X · bbX	Z · · · · · 1Z2 · · · · Z0000003Z

Optional Precision in Format

For decimal numbers, you may also add a period '.' followed by the number of decimal digits to display. This makes outputting currency and other decimal numbers much easier and more consistent.

Example

```
SELECT
    FORMAT('%s, %s', last_name, SUBSTR(first_name, 1, 1)) AS Name,
    FORMAT('%.2f', balance) AS Balance
    FROM owner
    JOIN ownerbalance
    ON owner.owner_id = ownerbalance.owner_id;
```

Format explained:

```
%s, %s
^^             string
  ^^           comma and space
    ^^         string
```

and

```
%.2f
^              fixed 2 decimal point
```

Name	Balance
Smithson, A	123.45
Greene, S	345.98

MSSQL Server

While MSSQL has a function named `FORMAT()`, it is very different in its function from the other databases. Additionally, it does not have a built-in way to do justification of strings so we will show other techniques that will allow you to do this.

Formatting a Decimal Number and Zero Fill

The `FORMAT()` function in MSSQL takes two or three arguments. The first is the value to be formatted, the second is a format code or mask, and the third is the optional locale for how to perform some common formatting tasks.[104]

Table 218: MSSQL Format Function

Function	Description
`FORMAT(expr, format_code)`	Format expression based on the formatting code supplied.
`FORMAT(expr, format_code, locale)`	Format expression based on the formatting code supplied for the supplied locale.

The following lists some of the more common format codes used by this function. For a detailed listing of the formats available, please see the documentation.[105]

- Integers
  - 'D' - Decimal Format Specifier
  - 'D#' - Zero fill an Integer to specified width
- Decimal
  - 'F' or 'F#' - Fixed decimal to local standard length (2) or to specified decimal places
  - 'E' - Exponential notation
  - 'G' - General Notation (either fixed or exponential)
  - 'N' or 'N#' - Number with separators with specified decimal places
  - 'C' - Number in currency format with currency symbol, separators, and specified decimal places

---

[104]https://learn.microsoft.com/en-us/sql/t-sql/functions/format-transact-sql?view=sql-server-ver16

[105]https://learn.microsoft.com/en-us/dotnet/standard/base-types/standard-numeric-format-strings

Example

Output a number right justified in 8 zeros, output a local currency value, output currency in France, and output a decimal number with 5 fixed decimal digits:

```
SELECT FORMAT(88, 'd8') AS ZFill,
    FORMAT(1234567.8,'C') AS USDollar,
    FORMAT(1234567.8,'C','fr-FR') AS 'French Euro',
    FORMAT(34567.898,'F5') AS Fixed5;
```

ZFill	USDollar	French Euro	Fixed5
00000088	$1,234,567.80	1 234 567,80 €	34567.89800

Padding Right and Left in Spaces

To pad a string with spaces on the left-hand side, you need to 1) prepend the spaces needed using the SPACE() function or 2) prepend too many spaces and use the RIGHT() function to trim it to size. The same process reversed can be used to pad spaces on the right-hand side.[106]

Table 220: MSSQL Space Function

Function	Description
SPACE(length)	Return a string of length spaces.

Example

Left justify the string 'foo' in 10 spaces and right justify the string 'bar' in 12 spaces:

```
SELECT LEFT('foo' + SPACE(10), 10) as Left10,
    RIGHT(SPACE(12) + 'bar', 12) as Right12;
```

Left10	Right12
foo · · · · · · ·	· · · · · · · · · bar

---

[106]https://learn.microsoft.com/en-us/sql/t-sql/functions/space-transact-sql?view=sql-server-ver16

Zero fill Right Justify

Zero filling may also be accomplished by prepending a string of zeros and then using the `RIGHT()` function to trim to size. The `REPLICATE()` function is an easy way to repeat a character multiple times in an expression.[107]

Table 222: MSSQL Replicate Function

Function	Description
`REPLICATE(expr, times)`	Repeat an expression specified number of times.

Example

Right justify the number 123 in a field of 8 zeros:

```
SELECT RIGHT(CONCAT(REPLICATE('0', 8), 123), 8) AS ZFill8;
```

ZFill8
00000123

Case

Using the Toy Store Order database we will answer a few more questions. The SQLite syntax was used for this case.

We are going to print shelf labels for our warehouse for each of the items that we sell. The label must be in all upper case and cannot be wider than 25 characters and needs the item_id, most of the name, and the first few letters of the vendor name.

```
SELECT UPPER(FORMAT('%5d %-13s %-5s', item_id,
    SUBSTR(description, 1, 13), SUBSTR(name, 1, 5) ) )
    AS LBL
    FROM item
    JOIN vendor ON item.vendor_id = vendor.vendor_id
    ORDER BY item_id;
```

LBL
1001 BLUE FLYING D ABC S
1002 RED FLYING DI ABC S
1003 RAINBOW FLYIN ABC S

---

[107]https://learn.microsoft.com/en-us/sql/t-sql/functions/replicate-transact-sql?view=sql-server-ver16

LBL
1004 GREY PRO FLYI ABC S
1010 YELLOW BUTTER FUN W
1011 BLUE ROYAL YO FUN W
1012 GIANT WOODEN FUN W
1018 PACK OF YO-YO FUN W
1019 YO-YO WAX FUN W
1020 CARDS AGAINST XYZ G
1022 GAME OF LIFE XYZ G
1023 NEVER ENDING XYZ G
1024 CLUELESS RISK XYZ G

List orders from September 2023 showing customer number, customer name, order number, and the order total with 2 decimal digits showing.

```
SELECT customer.customer_id, name,
    order_id, format('%.2f', total) AS total
    FROM order_header
    JOIN customer
    ON order_header.customer_id = customer.customer_id
    WHERE order_datetime LIKE '2023-09%'
    ORDER BY customer.customer_id, order_id;
```

customer_id	name	order_id	total
15	Adam Lewis	1156	182.69
17	Tiffany Branch	1409	253.98
18	Mega Big Box Store 101	1372	26.68
19	Aaron Blevins	1457	11.01
21	Jeffrey Hickman	1417	188.32
21	Jeffrey Hickman	1500	180.94
...	...	...	...
126	Todd Holt	1314	102.91
130	Trevor Smith	1024	65.86
130	Trevor Smith	1233	293.23
133	Toys-r-cool store 345	1399	121.63
134	Melissa Brown	1423	34.60

Exercises

Using the Media Collection database, answer the following questions.

1. We have decided it is time to attempt to sell off our entire album collection. We have purchased all the music we will ever want on a streaming service, and we need the room in our home. It is time to generate price labels for

the albums we still have. Create a single column with album_id, a space, the first 8 letters of the album name, another space and the cost * 2.75 nicely formatted.

2. We would like to create a nice listing of the movies that we have. List director name, movie name, year purchased, and cost. Only show the first 20 characters of the title.

Chapter 17 - SQL Attribute Logic

This chapter will show a few special functions and language expressions for handling column level logic. We can evaluate an expression and return values based upon the results.

Objectives

At the conclusion of this lesson module, students will be able to:

1. develop a case structure that will allow for logical operations in an attribute column.
2. use the `IF` or `IIF` function shortcut.
3. convert a NULL value to a default value in an expression.

CASE Expression

The `CASE` expression will evaluate an expression and return a value based on the results. There are two forms of `CASE`: 1) where it compares an expression to various simple expressions until it finds a match, and 2) where it evaluates each Boolean expression until it finds a true value.[108] [109] [110]

CASE with Simple Set

In the first form of the `CASE` expression, we will compare the expression to a list of values until we find a match. Once a match is found, the corresponding value will be returned. If no match is found, the optional `ELSE` value is returned or NULL is returned if `ELSE` was not specified.

Table 226: Case Expression - List of Values

Expression
CASE expr WHEN value1 THEN return1 WHEN value2 THEN return2 ... ELSE return_else END

Example

The veterinarian would like to show the common name for an animal's species and not the scientific name found in the 'species' table.

```
SELECT animal_id, name,
    CASE species_id
```

---

[108] https://www.sqlite.org/lang_expr.html#case
[109] https://dev.mysql.com/doc/refman/8.4/en/flow-control-functions.html#operator_case
[110] https://learn.microsoft.com/en-us/sql/t-sql/language-elements/case-transact-sql?view=sql-server-ver16

```
    WHEN 'C' THEN 'Cat'
    WHEN 'D' THEN 'Dog'
    ELSE 'Other' END AS Species
FROM animal
WHERE death_datetime IS NULL;
```

animal_id	name	Species
1	Kitty	Cat
3	Daisy	Cat
5	Cookie	Cat
6	Cookie	Dog
7	Penny	Cat
8	Holly	Cat
9	Rosie	Cat

CASE with Boolean Values

Evaluate Boolean expressions from left to right until a true value is found and return the associated value. This form has no expression between the CASE and WHEN keywords.

Table 228: Case Expression with Boolean Values

Expression
CASE WHEN bool_expr1 THEN return1 WHEN bool_expr2 THEN return2 ... ELSE return_else END

Example

In the veterinarian's office, we may want a column in a report that shows if an animal is small (0-7 pounds), medium(8-14 pounds) or large (15 pounds or larger).

Please note in the example below, if an animal weighs less than eight pounds, both the first and second condition are true. The value for the first boolean expression that evaluates to true is returned and evaluation stops.

```
SELECT animal_id, name, species_id,
    CASE WHEN weight < 8 THEN 'small'
        WHEN weight < 15 THEN 'medium'
        ELSE 'large' END AS Size
    FROM animal
    WHERE death_datetime IS NULL
    ORDER BY Size;
```

174

animal_id	name	species_id	Size
1	Kitty	C	large
7	Penny	C	large
5	Cookie	C	medium
6	Cookie	D	medium
3	Daisy	C	small
8	Holly	C	small
9	Rosie	C	small

IF or IIF Function

Each of the covered database implementations offer a shorthand for writing a simple `CASE` statement with one Boolean test. These functions perform the same operation as the `CASE WHEN x THEN y ELSE z END` expression except they are easier to write.[111] [112] [113] The table below shows the various forms of the `IF()` and `IFF()` functions and which database supports that syntax.

Table 230: If and Iif Functions

Function	Description	SQLite	MySQL	MSSQL
IF(x,y)	Return y if x is true else return NULL.	Yes		
IF(x,y,z)	Return y if x is true else return z.	Yes	Yes	
IIF(x,y)	Return y if x is true else return NULL.	Yes		
IIF(x,y,z)	Return y if x is true else return z.	Yes		Yes

Example - SQLite and MSSQL Server

Show a '*' beside the names of owners who have a balance. This can be done with an `IIF` because the balance column will contain a number or a `NULL` from the `LEFT JOIN`.

```
SELECT CONCAT_WS(' ', first_name, last_name,
    IIF(balance>0,'*','')) as 'Name*'
    FROM Owner
    LEFT JOIN ownerbalance
    ON owner.owner_id = ownerbalance.owner_id
    ORDER BY 'Name*';
```

---

[111] https://www.sqlite.org/lang_corefunc.html#iif

[112] https://dev.mysql.com/doc/refman/8.4/en/flow-control-functions.html#function_if

[113] https://learn.microsoft.com/en-us/sql/t-sql/functions/logical-functions-iif-transact-sql?view=sql-server-ver16

Name*
Amy Smithson *
Howard Ralston
John Clark
Lex Luton
Susan Greene *

IFNULL Function

The `IFNULL` function is another shortcut for the `CASE` expression. It does not exist in all SQL variants.

MySQL, MariaDB, and SQLite

The `IFNULL` function is used to simply change a NULL value into a not null value. As we have seen in prior chapters, any calculation with NULL always results in NULL being returned. Use this function, or the work-around for MSSQL when this behavior is not wanted.[114] [115]

Table 232: Ifnull Function

Function	Description
'IFNULL(x,y)'	Return y of x is NULL otherwise return x.

Example

For example, our veterinarian would like a report showing all animals, their age today or their age when they died, and a note that they are deceased.

SQLite

```
SELECT animal_id, name,
    ROUND( ( JULIANDAY(IFNULL(death_datetime, DATE('now') )) -
    JULIANDAY(birth_datetime) ) / 365.25, 1 ) AS Age,
    IF(death_datetime IS NULL,'','Deceased') AS Deceased
    FROM animal;
```

animal_id	name	Age	Deceased
1	Kitty	5.0	
2	Bobo	13.8	Deceased
3	Daisy	3.5	

---

[114]https://www.sqlite.org/lang_corefunc.html#iif
[115]https://dev.mysql.com/doc/refman/8.4/en/flow-control-functions.html#function_ifnull

animal_id	name	Age	Deceased
4	Bonnie	4.6	Deceased
5	Cookie	6.0	
6	Cookie	4.2	
7	Penny	6.5	
8	Holly	3.6	
9	Rosie	3.6	

MySQL

```
SELECT animal_id, name,
    ROUND( DATEDIFF(
    IFNULL(death_datetime, NOW() ),
    birth_datetime ) / 365.25, 1 ) AS Age,
    IF(death_datetime IS NULL,'','Deceased') AS Deceased
    FROM animal;
```

The output is the same as the SQLite version of the statement.

MSSQL Server

MSSQL Server does not have a function exactly like `IFNULL'`. It can easily be accomplished using an expression like`IIF(x IS NULL, y, x)`.

Case

Using the Media Collection database, we would like to list our artists by genre of their music. Artists #1, #2, #3, and #7 are "Rock"; #4, #5, and #6 are "Country"; #8 is "Folk"; and the others are "Unknown".

```
SELECT *,
    CASE WHEN artist_id = 1 OR artist_id = 2 OR artist_id = 3
    OR artist_id = 7 THEN 'Rock'
    WHEN artist_id >= 4 AND artist_id <= 6 THEN 'Country'
    WHEN artist_id = 8 THEN 'Folk'
    ELSE 'Unknown' END AS Genre
FROM artist;
```

artist_id	name	Genre
1	Motley Grunge	Rock
2	Queen Ant	Rock
3	Roach to Men	Rock
4	Taylor Slow	Country
5	George Wiggly	Country
6	Madison Tuckered	Country

artist_id	name	Genre
7	Purple Frog	Rock
8	Hazy Daisy	Folk
9	Frankie Ford Cooper	Unknown
10	Stanberg Cubic	Unknown
999	Various	Unknown

Alternatively it could have been written:

```
SELECT *,
    CASE artist_id WHEN 1 THEN 'Rock'
    WHEN 2 THEN 'Rock'
    WHEN 3 THEN 'Rock'
    WHEN 4 THEN 'Country'
    WHEN 5 THEN 'Country'
    WHEN 6 THEN 'Country'
    WHEN 7 THEN 'Rock'
    WHEN 8 THEN 'Folk'
    ELSE 'Unknown' END AS Genre
FROM artist;
```

Or even a third way as a series of nested IIF functions:

```
SELECT *,
    IIF(artist_id = 1, 'Rock', IIF(artist_id = 2, 'Rock',
    IIF(artist_id = 3, 'Rock', IIF(artist_id = 4, 'Country',
    IIF(artist_id = 5, 'Country', IIF(artist_id = 6, 'Country',
    IIF(artist_id = 7, 'Rock',
    IIF(artist_id = 8, 'Folk', 'Unknown' ))))))) AS Genre
FROM artist;
```

If I were to sell all the unsold albums with 100% markup, what would my total cost and sales be for all of my albums (sold and un-sold).

```
SELECT SUM(cost) AS TotalCost,
    SUM(IFNULL(price, cost*2)) as TotalSellingPrice
    FROM album;
```

TotalCost	TotalSellingPrice
410.5	841.93

Exercises

Answer the following with queries from the Toy Store Orders sample database.

1. Create a listing of customers from the state of "TX" showing name, and if they are a corporate store. Corporate stores have a billto customer.

2. Create a listing of items with item_id, description, price, and a sales price of 15% if the vendor is #2.

This page intentionally left blank.

Chapter 18 - SQL Maintain Tables and Indexes

In this chapter we will see how the general conceptual data types of fixed precision number, floating point number, string, Boolean value, datetime, and binary objects are implemented by each database. Then we will use these implemented types to create, edit, and remove tables from a database.

Objectives

At the conclusion of this lesson module, students will be able to:

1. list and describe the six generic data types of: fixed, float, string, Boolean, datetime, and BLOB.
2. identify the types in the various databases.
3. create, modify, and delete table definitions.
4. add primary and foreign keys to tables to enforce referential integrity.

Scenario Used in this Chapter

All the statement examples in this chapter will be used to create a database that will contain information about printers, either 2D or 3D.

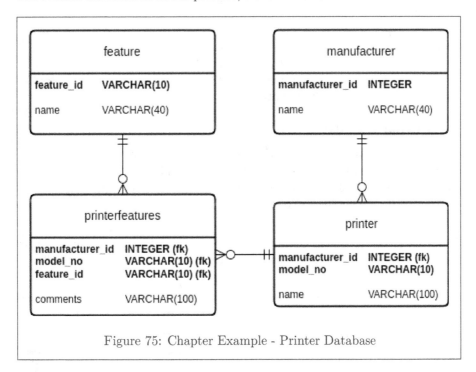

Figure 75: Chapter Example - Printer Database

A printer may be identified with a composite key made of the manufacturer ID concatenated to the model number. This way, if two manufacturers assign the same model number, they would still be unique printers. A surrogate key may have been added, but it was left out to make the creation of the tables more complex.

A printer may have many features (paper handling, format, speed, size, . . .) and may share the same features with other printers. An optional comment may be added to the feature on a specific printer.

Data Types

The phrase **data type** refers to the range or type an entity's attributes may contain. Each attribute in a table must be assigned a supported data type and the actual storage will be allocated by the database engine. Each database vendor may implement storage and specific data types differently.

Most databases implement these six common data types:

- Fixed precision number - like an integer or decimal number with a specified number of digits.
- Floating point number - a decimal approximation of a number also known as a real or double.
- String - a sequence of characters. Usually stored in the database engine as UTF-8 characters.
- Boolean - a true or false value.
- Date and Time - every database engine implements dates, times and timestamps differently, but they all handle this type of data.
- Binary Large Objects (BLOB)s - a BLOB is used to store binary files like images, sounds, encrypted attributes, or other non-text values.

MySQL and MariaDB

MySQL and MariaDB have implemented a vast collection of data types to use in your databases. Each type has limitations to size and precision. It is up to the database creator to choose a type large enough to store the valid range of the attribute without defining the column too large and wasting storage or network time.

The following table lists many of the most common data types in them. There are several others, please refer to the documentation for a complete list.[116]

Table 236: MySQL Common Data Types

Type	Description
BOOLEAN	True, false, 1, or 0.
INTEGER or INT	Integer Value (32 bit). -2,147,483,648 to 2,147,483,647 ($-2^{\hat{}}31$ to $2^{\hat{}}31$-1)
BIGINT	Big Integer Value (64 bit). -9,223,372,036,854,775,808 to 9,223,372,036,854,775,807 ($-2^{\hat{}}63$ to $2^{\hat{}}63$-1)
FLOAT(m,n)	Floating Point Number (7 significant decimal digits) m=digits, n=digits after decimal
DOUBLE(m,n)	Floating Point Number (15 to 17 significant decimal digits3) m=digits, n=digits after decimal
DECIMAL(m,n)	Fixed Point Decimal (Exact - 65 digits) m=digits, n=digits after decimal
VARCHAR(length)	Variable Character - string (specify maximum length)

[116]https://dev.mysql.com/doc/refman/8.0/en/data-types.html

Type	Description
TEXT	Text Attribute (0-216 in length)
BLOB	Binary Large Object (Image, Sound, or other Binary Data)
DATE	Date in ISO Format "YYYY-MM-DD"
DATETIME	Date and Time in ISO Format (24 Hour - seconds optional) "YYYY-MM-DD HH:MM:SS"

SQLite

The SQLite database is designed to be a low overhead embedded database that you can use in applications or on lower volume Web servers. Because of this intentional design, the SQLite database engine only implements five data types.[117]

Table 237: SQLite Data Types

Type	Description
NULL	The null value representing no value
INTEGER	Signed integer from -9,223,372,036,854,775,808 to 9,223,372,036,854,775,807 (-2^63 to 2^63-1). Also used for boolean values.
TEXT	Variable length text typically encoded as a UTF-8 string.
BLOB	Binary Large Object (Image, Sound, or other Binary Data)
REAL	Floating point number stored as an IEEE 64 bit Double-precision number (15-17 significant decimal digits)

When we are creating a database table you may use the names of most of the data types in other databases, but the database will actually use one of the data types above based on the value being saved in the attribute.

Because there is no specific date, time, or datetime data type in SQLite, dates may be stored in three ways:

1. as TEXT in ISO8601 format (YYYY-MM-DD HH:MM:SS.SSS or YYYY-MM-DDD),
2. as INTEGERS as Unix Time (number of seconds since 1970-01-01 00:00:00 UTC), or
3. as a REAL number of Julian days since Noon on November 24, 4714 BCE.

It is up to the database user/programmer to decide how they want to store dates and to validate them.

MSSQL Server

The MSSQL Server implements a robust set of data types for use in creating and maintaining tables.[118]

---

[117]https://www.sqlite.org/datatype3.html
[118]https://learn.microsoft.com/en-us/sql/t-sql/data-types/data-types-transact-sql?view=sql-server-ver16

Type	Description

Table 238: MySQL Common Data Types

Type	Description
BIT	A single bit 0 or 1 - Used for storing Boolean values. [119]
INT	Integer Value (32 bit). -2,147,483,648 to 2,147,483,647 (-2ˆ31 to 2ˆ31-1)
BIGINT	Big Integer Value (64 bit). -9,223,372,036,854,775,808 to 9,223,372,036,854,775,807 (-2ˆ63 to 2ˆ63-1)
MONEY	Fixed Point Decimal. [120] -922,337,203,685,477.5808 to 922,337,203,685,477.5807
FLOAT	Large floating Point Number.[121] -1.79E+308 to -2.23E-308, 0 and 2.23E-308 to 1.79E+308
REAL	Single precission floating Point Number. - 3.40E + 38 to -1.18E - 38, 0 and 1.18E - 38 to 3.40E + 38
NCHAR(length)	Fixed Length Character String (specify storage length) [122]
NVARCHAR(length)	Variable length Character - string (specify maximum length storage)
IMAGE	Variable length Binary Large Object (Image, Sound, or other Binary Data).[123]
DATE	Date in ISO Format "YYYY-MM-DD". [124]
DATETIME	Date and Time in ISO Format (24 Hour - seconds optional). [125] "YYYY-MM-DD HH:MM:SS.NNN"

CREATE TABLE

In SQL, we use the **CREATE TABLE** statement to create a new table in a database. It will allow us to name columns, specify data types for columns, define the primary and foreign keys, and set additional constraints.[126] [127] [128]

In the **CREATE TABLE** statement, the table name is followed by parenthesis with a comma separated list of attributes with their types and constraints followed by additional table level constraint information.

Table 239: Create Table Statement

Statement
`CREATE TABLE tablename ( colums_definitions and table_constraints );`

---

[119]https://learn.microsoft.com/en-us/sql/t-sql/data-types/bit-transact-sql?view=sql-server-ver16

[120]https://learn.microsoft.com/en-us/sql/t-sql/data-types/money-and-smallmoney-transact-sql?view=sql-server-ver16

[121]https://learn.microsoft.com/en-us/sql/t-sql/data-types/float-and-real-transact-sql?view=sql-server-ver16

[122]https://learn.microsoft.com/en-us/sql/t-sql/data-types/nchar-and-nvarchar-transact-sql?view=sql-server-ver16

[123]https://learn.microsoft.com/en-us/sql/t-sql/data-types/ntext-text-and-image-transact-sql?view=sql-server-ver16

[124]https://learn.microsoft.com/en-us/sql/t-sql/data-types/date-transact-sql?view=sql-server-ver16

[125]https://learn.microsoft.com/en-us/sql/t-sql/data-types/datetime-transact-sql?view=sql-server-ver16

[126]https://www.sqlite.org/lang_createtable.html

[127]https://dev.mysql.com/doc/refman/8.4/en/create-table.html

[128]https://learn.microsoft.com/en-us/sql/t-sql/statements/create-table-transact-sql?view=sql-server-ver16

This statement is extremely complex and this introduction shows a few simple use cases. For all of the available features, please see the documentation for your database.

Adding a Column

The first things that need defined in the **CREATE TABLE** statement are the columns themselves. Insert the column name followed by a space and the data type in the parenthesis. Use a comma separator between columns. You may also place column level constraints after the data type and before the next column.

Column Definition	Description
column type column_constraints	Column name, data type, and optional column level constraints.

Examples include:

- 'person_id INTEGER',
- 'address VARCHAR(40)',
- and 'order_datetime DATETIME'.

PRIMARY KEY Column Constraint

When you have a single attributes as the primary key, you may simply add **PRIMARY KEY** after the column type and the database will mark that field as the PK and will create an index on that attribute so that it may be retrieved rapidly.

The **NOT NULL** and **UNIQUE** column constraints automatically added to the definition of a primary key and can be omitted.

Table 241: PRIMARY KEY Column Constraint

Column Constraint	Description
column type **PRIMARY KEY**	Shortcut for a single attribute PK

NOT NULL Column Constraint

The **NOT NULL** table constraint tells the database not to allow NULL values to be inserted or updated in the column. This should be used on columns that are not part of the PK but need to be not NULL to enforce referential integrity. Columns may also be not NULL because their value is important and absolutely required by the application.

Table 242: NOT NULL Column Constraint

Column Constraint	Description
column type NOT NULL	Do not allow the NULL value in this attribute.

UNIQUE Column Constraint

If a column has the UNIQUE constraint, a value may only be inserted into the column once.

Table 243: UNIQUE Column Constraint

Column Constraint	Description
column type UNIQUE	Do not allow duplicate values in this attribute.

DEFAULT Column Constraint

The DEFAULT constraint is followed by an expression or constant value that is placed in a column if it is not included as a row is inserted.

Column Constraint	Description
column type DEFAULT expr	Default value if omitted from insert.

Adding Primary Key Table Constraint

The primary key may also be defined using the PRIMARY KEY table constraint. It will allow us to define either a single attribute key or a compound key as the primary key.

Table 245: Primary Key Constraint

Table Constraint	Description
PRIMARY KEY (column, ...)	Define one or more columns as the PK

Adding a Foreign Key Table Constraint

Foreign keys are defined on a table so that referential integrity can be maintained between tables. This means that a value in an foreign key column(s) needs to exist in the related table. We use the FOREIGN KEY table constraint to add this connection.

Table Constraint
`FOREIGN KEY (column, ...) REFERENCES table (remotecolumn, ...)`

The `FOREIGN KEY` constraint lists an attribute or attributes on the table we are creating, the name of the related table, and a list of the attribute(s) on the related table that make the connection. The attributes do not need to be named the same on the two tables, but they must be the same number and data type.

Examples

Now let us setup the printers database.

Manufacturer and Feature

Start by creating the control entities: manufacturer and feature. In the ERD, we defined the data types for each of the columns and have highlighted the single attributes that would be used a primary key.

```
CREATE TABLE manufacturer (
    manufacturer_id INTEGER PRIMARY KEY,
    name VARCHAR(40)
    );

CREATE TABLE feature (
    feature_id VARCHAR(10) PRIMARY KEY,
    name VARCHAR(40)
    );
```

Printer

The printer table adds the complexity of a ccompound primary key and a foreign key relationship back to the manufacturer table. Based on the ERD, the `PRIMARY KEY` constraint will need to contain both the manufacturer_id and model_no columns. We also need to add the `FOREIGN KEY` constraint connecting the manufacturer_id to the primary key on the manufacturer table.

```
CREATE TABLE printer (
    manufacturer_id INTEGER,
    model_no VARCHAR(10),
    name VARCHAR(100),
    PRIMARY KEY(manufacturer_id, model_no),
    FOREIGN KEY (manufacturer_id) REFERENCES
        manufacturer(manufacturer_id)
    );
```

PrinterFeatures

Lastly, we need to create the 'printerfeatures' table. It adds the complexity of three attributes being concatenated to form the composite primary key and two foreign key relationships.

```
CREATE TABLE printerfeatures (
    manufacturer_id INTEGER,
    model_no VARCHAR(10),
    feature_id VARCHAR(10),
    comments VARCHAR(255),
    PRIMARY KEY(manufacturer_id, model_no, feature_id),
    FOREIGN KEY (manufacturer_id, model_no) REFERENCES
        printer(manufacturer_id, model_no),
    FOREIGN KEY (feature_id) REFERENCES feature(feature_id)
);
```

DROP TABLE

The `DROP TABLE` statement is all you need to remove a table from a database.[129] [130] [131] It has the following general format:

Table 247: Drop Table Statement

Statement
`DROP TABLE tablename;`

WARNING

The `DROP TABLE` statement, if you have permissions and the relational rules in the database allow it, will permanently remove all data and the table from the database. There is no undo, except for restoring from a backup if you have one.

ALTER TABLE

After a table has been created, we may make alterations to it. These changes must be done carefully as to not break referential integrity or to cause saved `SELECT`, `INSERT INTO`, or `UPDATE` statements from continuing to work.

The `ALTER TABLE` is a complex statement that has different functionality based on the database engine. For additional functionality, please see the documentation

---

[129] https://www.sqlite.org/lang_droptable.html
[130] https://dev.mysql.com/doc/refman/8.4/en/drop-table.html
[131] https://learn.microsoft.com/en-us/sql/t-sql/statements/drop-table-transact-sql?view=sql-server-ver16

for your specific environment.[132] [133] [134]

Adding a Column

It often becomes necessary to add a new column to an existing table. Maybe a client wants to track an additional value or a requirement was missed in the original analysis. We use the `ADD COLUMN` clause to do this.

Table 248: Alter Table Statement - Add Column

Statement
`ALTER TABLE tablename ADD COLUMN column_name and  definition;`

Example

We would like to add a Manufacturer's Suggested Retail Price (MSRP) column to the printer table. The statement will create the column and set the new column on the existing rows to NULL.

```
ALTER TABLE printer ADD COLUMN msrp DECIMAL(12,2);
```

Dropping a Column

Dropping a column is as easy as using the `DROP COLUMN` clause. Like all other drops, extreme care must be taken when dropping a column. There is no undoing this in most environments.

Table 249: Alter Table Statement - Drop Column

Statement
`ALTER TABLE tablename DROP COLUMN columnname;`

Adding a Foreign Key Constraint

MySQL, MariaDB, and MSSQL Server

When you are adding tables and attribute to other tables, it often requires you to add a new constraint. The most common of these would be a new `FOREIGN KEY` constraint.

---

[132] https://www.sqlite.org/lang_altertable.html
[133] https://dev.mysql.com/doc/refman/8.4/en/alter-table.html
[134] https://learn.microsoft.com/en-us/sql/t-sql/statements/alter-table-transact-sql?view=sql-server-ver16

Table 250: Alter Table Statement - Add Foreign Key Constraint

Statement
`ALTER TABLE tablename ADD CONSTRAINT constraint_name FOREIGN KEY (column...) REFERENCES other_table(column...);`

SQLite

SQLite does not support adding a constraint to an existing table.

Dropping a Constraint

MySQL, MariaDB, and MSSQL Server

Dropping a constraint can also be accomplished using the `ALTER TABLE` statement. You will need to know the constraint name, which may have been assigned by the database.

Table 251: Alter Table Statement - Drop Constraint

Statement
`ALTER TABLE tablename DROP CONSTRAINT constraint_name;`

SQLite

SQLite does not support dropping a constraint from an existing table.

Indexing

An index, according to the Webster's dictionary is "a list usually arranged in alphabetical order of some specified datum".[135] An index can be created and automatically updated when records are inserted, changed or deleted. The index will be used to quickly select tables.

The database creates an index for the primary key, but to speed up searches on other fields, or groups of fields, we may need to create additional indexes.[136] [137] [138]

---

[135] https://www.merriam-webster.com/dictionary/index
[136] https://www.sqlite.org/lang_createindex.html
[137] https://dev.mysql.com/doc/refman/8.4/en/create-index.html
[138] https://learn.microsoft.com/en-us/sql/t-sql/statements/create-index-transact-sql?view=sql-server-ver16

Statement
CREATE INDEX indexname ON tablename (columns to index);
CREATE UNIQUE INDEX indexname ON tablename (columns to index);

There are several different options that may be used when creating an index, but the two most common ones are: 1) a general index and 2) a unique index. In a general index, duplicates may exist but in a unique index duplicate values for the index will cause an error. A UNIQUE index will permit multiple NULL values in MySQL and SQLite.[139]

Example

We would like to allow a quick lookup on email or on phone in our owner table. Several owners may share a phone number, but each owner must have a different email address. We would do this with the following statements:

```
CREATE INDEX owner_phone_index ON owner (phone);
CREATE UNIQUE INDEX owner_email_index ON owner (email);
```

Case

In this problem, we need to create a database for a company with a fleet of vehicles. The client specifically needs to track the accessories that have been installed or later uninstalled from vehicles.

Each vehicle has been assigned an integer vehicle number. Each technician also has been assigned a number to identify them. An accessory has a short alphanumeric code used in the process.

A Job is created when an accessory is installed on a vehicle by a technician. It contains the date and any comments the technician wants to add about the installation. If an accessory is later removed, for any reason, the original job is updated with when, who, and why it was removed.

The following ERD is a graphical representation of the problem.

---

[139]https://dev.mysql.com/doc/refman/8.4/en/create-index.html#create-index-unique

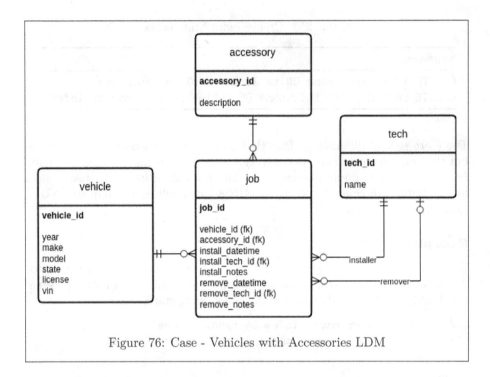

Figure 76: Case - Vehicles with Accessories LDM

Now let's create the actual database.

1) Create the accessory table, a categorical entity.

```
CREATE TABLE accessory (
    accessory_id VARCHAR(10) PRIMARY KEY,
    description VARCHAR(40)
    );
```

2) The technician table, that can be considered either a resource or categorical entity, needs to be created.

```
CREATE TABLE tech (
    tech_id INTEGER PRIMARY KEY,
    name VARCHAR(40)
    );
```

3) Now we can create the vehicle resource table. The owner has said that the usual state for licensing a vehicle is 'KY', so that has been set at the default for state. Also a 'vin' or Vehicle ID Number is on every vehicle and must be unique.

```
CREATE TABLE vehicle (
    vehicle_id INTEGER PRIMARY KEY,
    modelyear INTEGER,
    make VARCHAR(40),
```

```
   model VARCHAR(40),
   state VARCHAR(2) DEFAULT 'KY',
   license VARCHAR(10),
   vin VARCHAR(40) UNIQUE NOT NULL
   );
```

4) And now we create the job transaction table. A job must have an accessory, tech, and install datetime. The remove fields are left NULL until the product is later removed.

```
CREATE TABLE job (job_id INTEGER PRIMARY KEY,
   vehicle_id INTEGER NOT NULL,
   accessory_id VARCHAR(10) NOT NULL,
   install_datetime DATETIME NOT NULL,
   install_tech_id INTEGER NOT NULL,
   install_notes VARCHAR(256),
   remove_datetime DATETIME,
   remove_tech_id INTEGER,
   remove_notes VARCHAR(256),
   FOREIGN KEY (vehicle_id) REFERENCES vehicle(vehicle_id),
   FOREIGN KEY (accessory_id) REFERENCES accessory(accessory_id),
   FOREIGN KEY (install_tech_id) REFERENCES tech(tech_id),
   FOREIGN KEY (remove_tech_id) REFERENCES tech(tech_id)
   );
```

Exercises

For the following exercises, please use the ERD for a database of countries with regions and cities.

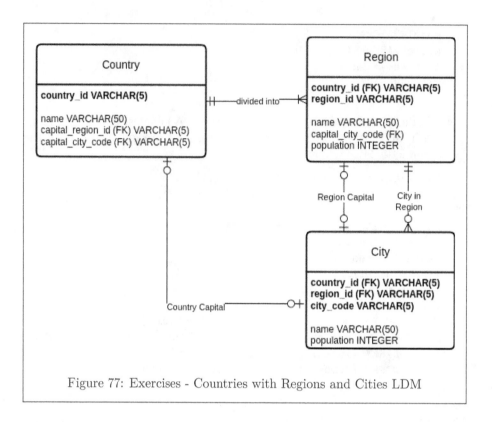

Figure 77: Exercises - Countries with Regions and Cities LDM

A country is made up one or more regions. For some countries, these regions may be called states or provinces, but the generic term region is being used. If there are no political regions in the country, one is added as a placeholder. A region may have zero or more cities and each city is assigned a unique code within the region. A city may be a regional capital or the capital for the entire country.

1. Create the Country table without the capital_city_code and capital_region_id attributes.

2. Create the Region table with the foreign key relationship to Country but without the capital_city_code attribute.

3. Create the City table with foreign key relationships to Country and Region.

4. Add the capital_city_code attribute to the Country table.

5. Add the capital_region_id attribute to the Country table.

6. Add the foreign key constraint for the capital city to the Country table. Skip if using an SQLite database.

7. Add the capital_city_code attribute to the Region table.

8. Add the foreign key constraint for the capital city to the Country table. Skip if using an SQLite database.

This page intentionally left blank.

Chapter 19 - SQL Inserting, Modifying, and Deleting Data

SQL databases would have little or no use if we could not add, modify, and delete data from the tables. This chapter will discuss how to perform these tasks. We will also be introduced to the concept of a transaction to make sure a group of changes will happen consistently.

Objectives

At the conclusion of this lesson module, students will be able to:

1. get a UUID or other unique identifier.
2. insert rows into a table.
3. update rows in a table.
4. delete rows from a table.
5. start a transaction.
6. commit or rollback a transaction.
7. perform an upsert in a table.

INSERT INTO

\index{INSERT INTO|see {SQL, Statement, INSERT INTO)} \index{VALUES|see {SQL, Clause, VALUES)} To add a new row to an entity, we will use the `INSERT INTO` statement.[140] [141]

Table 253: Insert Into Statement

Statement
`INSERT INTO table ( columns ) VALUES ( values );`
`INSERT INTO table VALUES ( values );`

The `INSERT INTO` statement has two basic forms: 1) with the column names listed, and 2) without them. It is preferred by most SQL users to not use the shortcut second form, because statements that worked in the past might stop working if the table structure is changed in any way.

In the first form, column names may be listed in any order, but the values must be listed in the same order. If you leave out columns, the `NULL` or default value will be inserted.

The second form, leaves off the column names. When this form is used, you must specify values for ALL columns in exactly the same order as displayed in a `SELECT * FROM` query. This is shorter to type but can lead to data problems if

---

[140] https://www.sqlite.org/lang_insert.html
[141] https://dev.mysql.com/doc/refman/8.4/en/insert.html

the table structure changes or if a simple mistake in the order of values was made. While this form is often used for quick ad hock inserts, it is not recommended for scripting or procedures.

Examples

For example, we have a new customer to add to our veterinarian's database. The `INSERT INTO` statement takes the table name, a list of the columns we will be filling, and the values to add to the entity.

```
INSERT INTO owner (owner_id, last_name, first_name, phone,
    email)
    VALUES (6, 'Jones', 'Arny', '555-555-5015',
    'arnyj88@notreal.com');
```

We can then do a `SELECT` to see that the record is now in the database.

```
SELECT * FROM owner WHERE owner_id = 6;
```

owner_id	last_name	first_name	phone	email
6	Jones	Arny	555-555-5015	arnyj88@notreal.com

In a second example, we do not know a new owner's phone number and we will leave it out of the list of attributes and values. Also notice that the order of attribute names and values is different than the previous example.

```
INSERT INTO owner (email, last_name, owner_id,
    first_name)
    VALUES ('soupy6@notreal.com', 'Sales', 7,
    'Soupy');
```

We can test that the new row was inserted correctly.

```
SELECT * FROM owner WHERE owner_id = 7;
```

owner_id	last_name	first_name	phone	email
7	Sales	Soupy	NULL	soupy6@notreal.com

In the third example, we can add another owner without specifying the column names.

```
INSERT INTO owner
    VALUES (8, 'Harris', 'Richard', 'rickyboi@notreal.com',
    '555-555-6632');
```

We can then do a `SELECT` to see that the record is in the database, but notice that we made a mistake and have reversed the email and phone number values.

```
SELECT * FROM owner WHERE owner_id = 8;
```

owner_id	last_name	first_name	phone	email
8	Harris	Richard	rickyboi@notreal.com	555-555-6632

UPDATE

\index{UPDATE|see {SQL, Statement, UPDATE}} \index{SET|see {SQL, Clause, SET}} The **UPDATE** statement is a powerful statement that uses the **WHERE** clause to update zero or more rows at the same time. When writing an **UPDATE** statement, you need to be extremely careful that the **WHERE** clause is correct. If it is in error, you may update rows you do not with too. You may omit the **WHERE** clause when you are updating all rows.[142] [143]

Table 257: Update Statement

Statement
UPDATE table SET field=value, ... WHERE selection;

Example

In the first example, let us correct the email address and phone number for owner #8.

```
UPDATE owner SET email = 'rickyboi@notreal.com',
    phone = '555-555-6632'
    WHERE owner_id = 8;
```

We can see the results of the update.

owner_id	last_name	first_name	phone	email
8	Harris	Richard	555-555-6632	rickyboi@notreal.com

DELETE FROM

\index{DELETE|see {SQL, Statement, DELETE}} The **DELETE FROM** statement does just what its name implies. An optional **WHERE** clause is used to select the rows to be deleted. This statement, like the **UPDATE**, can be dangerous if special care is not taken when writing the selection logic.

---

[142]https://www.sqlite.org/lang_update.html
[143]https://dev.mysql.com/doc/refman/8.4/en/update.html

If constraints are defined in the creation of the database tables, your database engine may not allow you to delete a row that would cause the foreign key relationship to be broken. In other constraint configurations, the deleting of a record on one table can cause automatic deletes of related records on other records.[144] [145]

Table 259: Delete From Statement

Statement
DELETE FROM table WHERE selection;

Example

We want to delete owner #7 from the veterinarian's database.

```
DELETE FROM owner WHERE owner_id = 7;
```

Get a Universally Unique Identifier (UUID)

Often when we are inserting a transaction into a database table, we don't care what its primary key is. It just needs to have one. This is especially true where transactions may be coming from multiple sources and will eventually be brought together into a single repository. To solve this problem, the concept of the Universally Unique Identifier (UUID) was created.

A UUID is a 128 bit sequence that is typically made up of your network adapter's serial number, the UNIX epoch time, and a large random number. Because of the complexity and length of a UUID, it is virtually impossible for two identical ones to be issued and used in the same application.

But like so many things, each database vendor has a different function to generate them.

MySQL and MariaDB

In MySQL, the UUID() function will generate and return a UUID.[146] The UUID will be a string in the standard hexadecimal format of 'aaaaaaaa-bbbb-cccc-dddd-eeeeeeeeeeee'.

---

[144]https://www.sqlite.org/lang_delete.html
[145]https://dev.mysql.com/doc/refman/8.4/en/delete.html
[146]https://dev.mysql.com/doc/refman/8.4/en/miscellaneous-functions.html#function_uuid

Table 260: Create a UUID - MySQL

Function	Description
UUID()	Return a UUID.

Example

Get a new UUID. We usually will be using this function in an INSERT INTO for a primary key column.

SELECT UUID();

UUID()
4049e9fe-e249-11ef-8487-047c16fd53a0

SQLite

SQLite does not have a builtin function to generate UUIDs. The SQLite documentation suggests generating a 128 bit (16 byte) long BLOB and using that as a UUID. The recommended expression is LOWER(HEX(RANDOMBLOB(16))).[147]

Table 262: Create a UUID - SQLite

Function	Description
LOWER(HEX(RANDOMBLOB(16)))	Return a UUID.

If we look at the expression, we can see the RANDOMBLOB() function creates a 16 byte (128 bit) long random block of bytes, the HEX() statement converters the BLOB to an uppercase string of hexadecimal characters, and lastly the LOWER() function changes the letters A-F to lower case. It does not contain the dashes that often exist in a UUID.

Function	Description
RANDOMBLOB(length)	Create a random BLOB of length bytes
HEX(blob)	Return a hexadecimal string of the bytes in a BLOB

---

[147]https://www.sqlite.org/lang_corefunc.html#randomblob

Example

Generate a random sequence that can be used an a UUID.

```
SELECT LOWER(HEX(RANDOMBLOB(16)));
```

LOWER(HEX(RANDOMBLOB(16)))
0c2e69202946a75621d0fa534e38d787

MSSQL Server

The `NEWID()` function creates a new UUID.[148]

Table 265: Create a UUID - MSSQL

Function	Description
NEWID()	Return a UUID.

Example

Create a UUID in MSSQL.

```
SELECT NEWID();
```

(No column name)
f63b3e29-2e90-43d4-80b3-f8a2e243265d

Transactions

Transactions are a way of grouping multiple SQL statements into a single update to the database. These transactions may affect multiple rows and multiple tables. A transaction makes sure that all the changes happen at the same time and allows for the transaction to be cancelled (rolled back) if an error happens during one step in the process.

MySQL and MariaDB

Statement	Description
START TRANSACTION;	Start a transaction.[149]
COMMIT;	Close transaction and update all changes.
ROLLBACK;	Close transaction but undo any changes.

Table: MySQL Transaction Statements

---

[148] https://learn.microsoft.com/en-us/sql/t-sql/functions/newid-transact-sql?view=sql-server-ver16

[149] https://dev.mysql.com/doc/refman/8.4/en/commit.html

SQLite and MSSQL Server

| Statement | Description | | | ————- | —————————————————
— | | BEGIN TRANSACTION; | Start a transaction.[150] [151] | | COMMIT; | Close transaction and update all changes. | | ROLLBACK; | Close transaction but undo any changes. | Table: SQLite and MSSQL Transaction Statements

Example

As an example in the veterinarian's database, we want to post a new charge to animal #9, right now, for the amount of $35.67, to purchase flea drops. To do this, we need to create a charge record and at the same time create a new balance record for owner (#5). If the owner already had a record on the 'ownerbalance' table, we would need to update the balance not insert a new row (see UPSERT).

MySQL Version

```
START TRANSACTION;
INSERT INTO charges (charge_uuid, animal_id,
    charge_datetime, description, amount)
    VALUES
    (UUID(), 8,
    NOW(), 'flea drop', 35.67);
INSERT INTO ownerbalance (owner_id, balance)
    VALUES
    (5, 35.67);
COMMIT;
```

SQLite Version

```
BEGIN TRANSACTION;
INSERT INTO charges (charge_uuid, animal_id,
    charge_datetime, description, amount)
    VALUES
    (LOWER(HEX(RANDOMBLOB(16))), 8,
    DATETIME('now'), 'flea drop', 35.67);
INSERT INTO ownerbalance (owner_id, balance)
    VALUES
    (5, 35.67);
COMMIT;
```

MSSQL Version

---

[150] https://learn.microsoft.com/en-us/sql/t-sql/language-elements/begin-transaction-transact-sql?view=sql-server-ver16

[151] https://www.sqlite.org/lang_transaction.html

```
BEGIN TRANSACTION;
INSERT INTO charges (charge_uuid, animal_id,
    charge_datetime, description, amount)
    VALUES
    (NEWID(), 8,
    GETDATE(), 'flea drop', 35.67);
INSERT INTO ownerbalance (owner_id, balance)
    VALUES
    (5, 35.67);
COMMIT;
```

UPSERT - Update or Insert

There will be times when you will want to INSERT a new record or make an UPDATE if a record already exists, This is commonly called an UPSERT. There is no standard syntax across databases, and it can often be accomplished in several different ways with a single database.

MySQL and MariaDB

In MySQL, you may add the special clause ON DUPLICATE KEY UPDATE' followed by attribute assignments to theINSERT INTO' statement. When the insert would otherwise fail for a duplicated primary key, the update logic will execute for the existing single row.[152]

Table 267: MySQL UPSERT Clause

Clause	Description
ON DUPLICATE KEY UPDATE column=value, ...	Columns to update if the row already exists

Example

The following example continues to refine adding a charge to an animal and updating an owner's balance. We see if an owner does not have a balance in the ownerbalance table it is added with the amount, otherwise the balance is increased by the charge amount.

```
START TRANSACTION;

INSERT INTO charges (charge_UUid, animal_id,
    charge_datetime, description, amount)
    VALUES
    (UUID(), 6,
```

---

[152]https://dev.mysql.com/doc/refman/8.4/en/insert-on-duplicate.html

```
    NOW(), 'weight control food', 29.97);

INSERT INTO ownerbalance
    (owner_id, balance) VALUES (4, 29.97)
    ON DUPLICATE KEY UPDATE
    balance = balance + 29.97;

COMMIT;
```

SQLite

UPSERT is handled in SQLite by adding one or more **ON CONFLICT** clause on the end of an **INSERT INTO** statement.[153] If a uniqueness conflict is detected, you may either trigger an **UPDATE** or you may tell the database to do **NOTHING** and ignore the conflict.

Table 268: SQLite UPSERT Clauses

Clause
ON CONFLICT (uniqueness_constraint,...) DO UPDATE SET column=value, ...
ON CONFLICT (uniqueness_constraint,...) DO NOTHING

There may be several **ON CONFLICT** clauses and if any of the uniqueness constraints fail the corresponding **DO** clause will execute on the row. The uniqueness constraint may be left off of the last **ON CONFLICT** clause and will trigger when an unhandled conflict occurs.

Examples

The following transaction refines the process of adding a charge to an animal and updating an owner's balance. If an owner does not have a balance in the ownerbalance table, a new row is inserted, otherwise a conflict is detected and the balance is updated with the charge amount.

```
BEGIN TRANSACTION;

INSERT INTO charges (charge_id, animal_id,
    charge_datetime, description, amount)
    VALUES
    (LOWER(HEX(RANDOMBLOB(16))), 6,
    DATETIME('now'), 'weight control food', 29.97);

INSERT INTO ownerbalance
```

---

[153]https://www.sqlite.org/lang_upsert.html

```
    (owner_id, balance) VALUES (4, 29.97)
    ON CONFLICT DO UPDATE SET
    balance = balance + 29.97;
```

```
COMMIT;
```

This could also be accomplished by using an INSERT INTO with the ON CONFLICT DO NOTHING clause to always try to add a balance of zero if it does not exist. Once it is created, if needed, we would use the UPDATE to actually increase the balance.

```
BEGIN TRANSACTION;
```

```
INSERT INTO charges (charge_id, animal_id,
    charge_datetime, description, amount)
    VALUES
    (LOWER(HEX(RANDOMBLOB(16))), 6,
    DATETIME('now'), 'weight control food', 29.97);
```

```
INSERT INTO ownerbalance
    (owner_id, balance) VALUES (4, 0)
    ON CONFLICT DO NOTHING;
```

```
UPDATE ownerbalance SET
    balance = balance + 29.97
    WHERE owner_id = 4;
```

```
COMMIT;
```

MSSQL Server

Unlike the other two databases, MSSQL Server does not have a special clause for the INSERT INTO statement to perform an UPSERT.[154] There are several different ways to perform this operation using error trapping, the IF statement, and embedded statements.

One easy to understand method for doing an UPSERT is to attempt to do an UPDATE and if no rows are found to update then perform the INSERT INTO. This can be accomplished by using MSSQL's IF statement with the system function @@ROWCOUNT.[155] [156]

---

[154]https://michaeljswart.com/2017/07/sql-server-upsert-patterns-and-antipatterns
[155]https://learn.microsoft.com/en-us/sql/t-sql/language-elements/if-else-transact-sql?view=sql-server-ver16
[156]https://learn.microsoft.com/en-us/sql/t-sql/functions/rowcount-transact-sql?view=sql-server-ver16

Table 269: MSSQL IF Statement

Statement	Description
IF expression statement;	Execute statement if expression is true.

The **IF** statement is a complex statement that can execute a single statement or block of statements if an expression is true. It may also be followed by an **ELSE** clause with a statement or block of statements that are executed when the condition is false. Please see the documentation for details.

Table 270: MSSQL @@ROWCOUNT System Function

Function	Description
@@ROWCOUNT	Returns number of rows affected by the last SQL statement.

Example

In the transaction to post a charge to an animal and update the owner's balance we attempt an **UPDATE** to increase the balance due. If the row exists **@@ROWCOUNT** will be 1, but if the row does not exist it will be 0. The third statement in the transaction will insert the new balance if there was not a previous balance to update.

```
BEGIN TRANSACTION;

INSERT INTO charges (charge_id, animal_id,
    charge_datetime, description, amount)
    VALUES
    (NEWID(), 6,
    GETDATE(), 'weight control food', 29.97);

UPDATE ownerbalance
    SET balance = balance + 29.97
    WHERE owner_id = 4;

IF (@@ROWCOUNT = 0)
    INSERT INTO ownerbalance
        (owner_id, balance) VALUES (4, 29.97)   ;

COMMIT;
```

Case

For our case, we will insert some sample data into the vehicle accessories database that we created in the previous chapter.

1) Insert our technicians into the database.

```
INSERT INTO tech VALUES (1,'Bobby Wrench');
INSERT INTO tech VALUES (2,'Willie Jack');
INSERT INTO tech VALUES (3,'Henrietta Hammer');
```

2) Now add accessories that we will be installing on our vehicles.

```
INSERT INTO accessory VALUES ('FD','Fuzzy Dice');
INSERT INTO accessory VALUES ('YFL','Yellow Flashing Light');
INSERT INTO accessory VALUES ('MUD','Mud Flaps');
INSERT INTO accessory VALUES ('HO','Hood Ornament');
```

3) Now add the vehicles from our motor-pool to the database. Notice that some of the inserts do not include the 'state' column and the default value will be inserted.

```
INSERT INTO vehicle (vehicle_id, modelyear, make,
    model, license, vin)
    VALUES (1, 2023, 'GMC', 'Sierra',
    'KJH654', '88UY654RE876543');
INSERT INTO vehicle (vehicle_id, modelyear, make,
    model, license, vin)
    VALUES (2, 1968, 'AMC', 'Rambler American',
    'AJX123', '76GH543CV765765');
INSERT INTO vehicle (vehicle_id, modelyear, make,
    model, state, license, vin)
    VALUES (3, 1993, 'VOLVO', '240 DL',
    "OH", '987YHG', '44FE543PP556677');
INSERT INTO vehicle (vehicle_id, modelyear, make,
    model, license, vin)
    VALUES (4, 2023, 'GMC', 'Sierra',
    'KJH664', '88UY654RE876876');
```

4) Now add a few jobs.

```
INSERT INTO job (job_id, vehicle_id, accessory_id,
    install_datetime, install_tech_id, install_notes )
    VALUES
    ( 1, 1, 'YFL', '2024-11-01 13:02', 1, 'On roof' );
INSERT INTO job (job_id, vehicle_id, accessory_id,
    install_datetime, install_tech_id, install_notes )
    VALUES
    ( 2, 4, 'YFL', '2024-11-01 14:45', 1, 'On roof' );
INSERT INTO job (job_id, vehicle_id, accessory_id,
```

```
    install_datetime, install_tech_id )
    VALUES
    ( 3, 2, 'FD', '2024-11-02 09:23', 2 );
INSERT INTO job (job_id, vehicle_id, accessory_id,
    install_datetime, install_tech_id, install_notes,
    remove_datetime, remove_tech_id, remove_notes ) VALUES
    ( 4, 1, 'FD', '2024-11-01 16:40', 1, NULL,
    '2024-11-02', 3, 'blocked driver vision' );
```

5) Now let us post that we had Henrietta remove the fuzzy dice from vehicle #2 because they were the wrong scent and that the driver was allergic to the smell.

```
UPDATE job SET remove_datetime = '2024-12-03 13:55',
    remove_tech_id = 3,
    remove_notes = 'driver sensitive to smell'
    WHERE job_id = 3;
```

Exercises

Insert the following data into the Country database created in the previous chapter.

Table 271: Country Data to Insert

country_id	name	capital_region_id	capital_city_code
AD	Principality of Andorra	ALL	ALV
CA	Canada	NULL	NULL
US	United States of America	DC	WAS

Table 272: Region Data to Insert

country_id	region_id	name	population	capital_city_code
AD	ALL	Whole Country	81938	ALV
CA	ON	Ontario	16124116	NULL
US	AZ	Arizona	7431000	NULL
US	DC	District of Columbia	678972	WAS
US	KY	Kentucky	4526000	FRK
US	VA	Virginia	8716000	RCH

Table 273: City Data to Insert

country_id	region_id	city_code	name	population
AD	ALL	ALV	Andorra la Vella	20719
US	DC	WAS	Washington	678972
US	KY	FRK	Frankfort	28285
US	KY	LEX	Lexington	320154
US	VA	LEX	Lexington	7528
US	VA	RCH	Richmond	229247

1. Insert the country data but leave capital_region_id and capital_city_code NULL.

2. Insert the region data but leave capital_city_code NULL.

3. Insert the city data.

4. Update four regions with their capital city code.

5. Update two countries with their capital_region_id and capital_city_code.

Chapter 20 - SQL Subqueries

For even more flexibility, SQL allows us to use a query with another query. we call these, subqueries. This chapter will show several common uses for them.

Objectives

At the conclusion of this lesson module, students will be able to:

1. use the IN operator in a WHERE clause with either a list of values or a subquery.
2. use a subquery in the FROM clause of a SELECT statement.
3. create a UNION of two tables to report on data from multiple sources.
4. insert a recordset into a table using INSERT INTO SELECT.

IN Operator

A common use of a subquery is in the WHERE clause. There is a special operator, called IN, that accepts a list or a recordset of values from a subquery.[157] [158] If the tested field is in the list, then a true value will be returned.

Table 274: In Operator

Operator	Description
expression IN (list, ...)	Return true if expression is found in list of values.
expression IN (SELECT ...)	Return true if expression is found in result of sub-query.

Examples

We can write the query to see all neutered animals using the IN operator and a list of values:

```
SELECT animal_id, owner_id, gender_id
    FROM animal WHERE gender_id IN ('NM', 'NF');
```

animal_id	owner_id	species_id
1	1	C
2	1	D
3	3	C
4	3	C

---

[157] https://www.sqlite.org/lang_expr.html#in_op
[158] https://dev.mysql.com/doc/refman/8.4/en/comparison-operators.html#operator_in

211

animal_id	owner_id	species_id
5	3	C
6	4	D
7	5	C
8	5	C
9	5	C

We can rewrite this using a subquery as the list for the IN operator. The subquery SELECT gender_id FROM gender WHERE description LIKE 'neutered%' returns a list of gender_ids that start with the word 'neutered'. It will return a list of 'NM' and 'NF' unless an additional neutered type was added to the table. Be sure to write your subquery to return a list of values (not entire rows) to use in the compare process.

```
SELECT animal_id, owner_id, gender_id
    FROM animal WHERE gender_id
    IN (
        SELECT gender_id FROM gender
        WHERE description LIKE 'neutered%'
    );
```

While this example is much more complex that the original statement using a defined list of values, it shows the power of a subqurery. A subquery works best if the list of values was long or if the list changes from time to time.

FROM Source or in a JOIN

Queries can also be used in a **FROM** or **JOIN** as a virtual table. Be sure to use the **AS** clause to alias the recordset in joins and complex queries. This is especially useful when you need an aggregated value from a table to compare with another.

Example

Our veterinarian wants to find all living cats who are probably obese. The criteria the vet wants to use is that any cat that weights 150% of the average weight of all cats should be listed. We could do a query to calculate the target weight and use that value in a subsequent select.

But let's do it with a subquery. In the query below, we are creating a dot product of a single value (the target weight - w.target) and the entire table of animals. Then in the **WHERE** clause we are selecting the animals that weigh more than the target.

```
SELECT animal_id, owner_id, name, weight
    from (SELECT AVG(weight)*1.5 AS target FROM animal
        WHERE species_id = 'C') as w,
        animal
```

```
WHERE weight > w.target
AND death_datetime IS NULL
AND species_id = 'C';
```

animal_id	owner_id	name	weight
1	1	Kitty	17.0
7	5	Penny	15.0

Expression

Subqueries may also appear virtually anywhere an attribute or an expression can be used. When doing this, your recordset should contain exactly one value. Put the query in parenthesis. Be sure to alias the expression.

Example

In the following example, we can see a list of owners with the count of animals that they have in the database. The same result can be accomplished with a JOIN and GROUP BY but often this is an effective way to create complex queries.

```
SELECT owner_id, last_name, first_name,
    (SELECT COUNT(*) FROM animal
        WHERE animal.owner_id = owner.owner_id) AS Animals
    FROM owner;
```

owner_id	last_name	first_name	Animals
1	Smithson	Amy	2
2	Ralston	Howard	0
3	Greene	Susan	3
4	Luton	Lex	1
5	Clark	John	3

Union

A UNION takes two queries and merges the recordsets. This is especially useful when reporting or summarizing data from multiple sources. In order to be able to do this operation, the two recordsets need to be **union compatible**. This means that they must have the same number of columns and that the columns should be of the same type.[159] [160]

---

[159]https://www.sqlite.org/lang_select.html#compound_select_statements
[160]https://dev.mysql.com/doc/refman/8.4/en/union.html

statement	Description
recordset UNION recordset	Merge two recordsets, removing duplicate rows.
recordset UNION ALL recordset	Merge two recordsets together, preserving duplicate rows.

The `UNION` conjunction will eliminate duplicate rows. You may use the `UNION ALL` variant to return all rows, even duplicate ones.

Example

Using the Media Collection database, we would like to create a single list of movies and albums for artist #4 'Taylor Slow'. We want the first column to contain a letter 'A' or 'M' showing if it was an album or movie. The second and third columns should show the title and year.

```
SELECT 'A' AS type, album_title AS title, year
    FROM album
    WHERE artist_id = 4
UNION
    SELECT 'M', title, year FROM movie
    WHERE director_id = 4;
```

Table 279: UNION Result

type	title	year
A	Celestial Canvas	1981
A	Greatest Hits	2020
A	Nebula Reverie	1976
A	Solar Symphony	1970
A	Velvet Twilight	1974
M	21 Days After	2000
M	Error Concert Tour Highlights	2025

See the `INSERT INTO SELECT` example for another `UNION`.

INSERT INTO SELECT Statement

In the `INSERT INTO` statement, the results of a `SELECT` statement may be used instead of the `VALUES` clause. This allows a selected recordset to be inserted into another table. This is often used to restructure a table by creating a table in the new format and then selecting the rows and columns to be moved. It also is often used to initially build or rebuild tables that contain totals.

Table 280: Insert Into Select Statement

Statement
`INSERT INTO table (columns) SELECT ...;`
`INSERT INTO table SELECT ...;`

Example

In the veterinarian's office database, there is a table called 'ownerbalance' that contains the running balance for each owner. This has a "one to zero or one" relationship with 'owner' and could have been implemented as a balance attribute on the 'owner' table. If the 'ownerbalance' table would be corrupt or for some other reason we needed to rebuild it, the following statement would do it:

```
INSERT INTO ownerbalance
    SELECT owner_id, SUM(amount) FROM (
        SELECT owner_id, amount
            FROM charges
            JOIN animal ON animal.animal_id = charges.animal_id
        UNION ALL
        SELECT owner_id, amount*-1
            FROM payments ) candp
    GROUP BY owner_id;
```

This statement uses two inner subqueries to create a recordset of owner's with charges and another with owner's payments (as a negative). The `UNION ALL` statement joins those two recordsets together. That new set is used as the FROM into another **SELECT** statement to group by owner and total the charges and payments into a new balance. We now have a simple recordset of just owner_id and balance to insert into the 'ownerbalance' table.

Case

We will be using the GeneralLedger sample database to answer several business questions.

Generate a list of the Asset, Liability, and Capital accounts that make up a simple balance sheet for company 1.

```
SELECT accounttype_id, account.account_id, description, balance
    FROM accountbalance
    JOIN account ON accountbalance.account_id = account.account_id
    WHERE accounttype_id IN ('A', 'L', 'C')
    AND company_id = 1;
```

accounttype_id	account_id	description	balance
A	100	Cash	489.00
A	110	Accounts Receivable	23.00
A	190	Inventory	1180.00
L	200	Accounts Payable	-750.00
C	300	Shareholder Equity	-1000.00

Calculate the current retained earnings for company #1 by creating the total of the accounts that are not type 'A', 'L', or 'C'.

```
SELECT SUM(balance)
    FROM accountbalance
    JOIN account ON accountbalance.account_id = account.account_id
    WHERE accounttype_id NOT IN ('A', 'L', 'C')
    AND company_id = 1;
```

(No column name)
58.00

Add columns to make the retained earnings recordset union compatible (use account number 399 and description 'Current Retained Earnings') and add it to the recordset of the other balance sheet accounts.

```
SELECT accounttype_id, account.account_id, description, balance
    FROM accountbalance
    JOIN account ON accountbalance.account_id = account.account_id
    WHERE accounttype_id IN ('A', 'L', 'C')
    AND company_id = 1
UNION
SELECT 'C','399','Current Retained Earnings', SUM(balance)
    FROM accountbalance
    JOIN account ON accountbalance.account_id = account.account_id
    WHERE accounttype_id NOT IN ('A', 'L', 'C')
    AND company_id = 1;
```

accounttype_id	account_id	description	balance
A	100	Cash	489.00
A	110	Accounts Receivable	23.00
A	190	Inventory	1180.00
C	300	Shareholder Equity	-1000.00
C	399	Current Retained Earnings	58.00
L	200	Accounts Payable	-750.00

Use the recordset from the UNION as a source in a SELECT, make the column headers meaningful and sort the output by account number.

```
SELECT *
    FROM (
        SELECT accounttype_id AS Type,
        account.account_id as Account,
        description AS 'Account Name',
        balance as 'Balance'
        FROM accountbalance
        JOIN account
        ON accountbalance.account_id = account.account_id
        WHERE accounttype_id IN ('A', 'L', 'C')
        AND company_id = 1
    UNION
    SELECT 'C','399','Current Retained Earnings',
        SUM(balance)
        FROM accountbalance
        JOIN account
        ON accountbalance.account_id = account.account_id
        WHERE accounttype_id NOT IN ('A', 'L', 'C')
        AND company_id = 1
) BS
ORDER BY Account;
```

Type	Account	Account Name	Balance
A	100	Cash	489.00
A	110	Accounts Receivable	23.00
A	190	Inventory	1180.00
L	200	Accounts Payable	-750.00
C	300	Shareholder Equity	-1000.00
C	399	Current Retained Earnings	58.00

The 'accountbalance' table contains the balance for each company's account. We have detected an error in that table and need to empty it and rebuild.

```
DELETE FROM accountbalance;

INSERT INTO accountbalance
    SELECT company_id, account_id, SUM(amount) AS balance
    FROM ledgertransactiondetail
    JOIN ledgertransaction
    ON ledgertransactiondetail.transaction_uuid =
        ledgertransaction.transaction_uuid
    GROUP BY company_id, account_id;
```

Exercises

Use the Media Collection sample database for the following exercises.

1. Create a query that returns a list of song_id numbers on albums by artist_id 999 (join album and album_track). Use this query in an IN clause to list song_id and title from the song table.

2. Create a single list of albums and movies we have sold. List a media Type constant of 'A' or 'M' for which table the row came from, the title, the cost, the date purchased, the selling price, and the date sold.

3. We would like to sort the previous UNION by date sold. To do this, take the UNION from the previous assignment and use it as a record source for a new SELECT.

Chapter 21 - SQL Variables and Stored Procedures

This chapter will go into details about stored procedures and functions. These allow you to write reusable blocks of complex SQL code to standardize how things are done and to reduce errors. Variables, an important part of creating procedures and functions, will also be shown.

Objectives

At the conclusion of this lesson module, students will be able to:

1. create and alter a variable or parameter.
2. use basic variables as parameters in SQL statements.
3. create, alter, and drop a stored procedure.
4. use basic variables in a stored procedure to collect parameters and calculate values to be returned.
5. execute/call a stored procedure.
6. create and call a stored function.

Variables

Variables and statement parameters are implemented by the database providers differently. Please see the sections for each individual database.

MySQL and MariaDB

MySQL includes a powerful feature that allows the SQL programmer to set and use variables in their queries.[161] A variable is what its name implies, it represents a named block of the server's memory that stores a value that can be retrieved with the name.

In MySQL, variable names should be prefixed with the @ symbol and should have a name made of letters [a-z], numbers [0-9], and underscores. Variable names are case-insensitive, the variable @Ab_11 is the same as @aB_101.

Set a Variable

MySQL allows for a variable to be set in several ways. Some of the commonly used ways are shown.

Using the SET Statement

The easiest and first method to set a variable is to use the SET statement. This statement will create a new variable or reassign a variable once it is executed.

---

[161]https://dev.mysql.com/doc/refman/8.4/en/set-variable.html

Table 285: MySQL Set Statement

Statement	Description
SET @variable := expression;	Set the variable with the expression.

The := operator must be used in assignment to keep it from being confused with the equal to = operation.

Example

We can set variables with specific values or even with the results of another statement:

```
SET @invoice := 12345;
SET @userName := 'Lex';
SET @num_live_animals := (SELECT count(*)
    FROM animal WHERE death_datetime IS NULL);

SELECT @invoice, @USERNAME, @NUM_LIVE_animals;
```

@invoice	@USERNAME	@NUM_LIVE_animals
12345	Lex	7

Setting in a SELECT Statement

Setting from a SELECT statement may be accomplished in one of two ways: 1) using the assignment operator := or 2) using the INTO keyword.[162] [163]

Example

Set the variable 'outstanding' to the total of all owner's balances.

```
SELECT @outstanding := SUM(balance) FROM ownerbalance;
```

@outstanding := SUM(balance)
469.43

Set the variable 'num_owners' to the number of all owners and the variable 'total_balance' to the sum of the balances.

---

[162] https://dev.mysql.com/doc/refman/8.4/en/assignment-operators.html#operator_assign-value

[163] https://dev.mysql.com/doc/refman/8.4/en/select-into.html

```
SELECT COUNT(*), SUM(balance) INTO @num_owners,
    @total_balance FROM owner
    LEFT JOIN ownerbalance
    ON owner.owner_id = ownerbalance.owner_id;

SELECT @num_owners, @total_balance;
```

@num_owners	@total_balance
5	469.43

SQLite

SQLite does not implement a true variable like many other databases do. There is a simple mechanism in the Command Line Interface (CLI) for the creation of parameters, assigning them values, and using the parameters in your SQL statements.[164] [165]

MSSQL Server

MSSQL Server also includes a robust feature of being able to declare, set, reset and use variables. A variable is what its name implies, it represents a named block of the server's memory that stores a value that can be retrieved with the name.[166]

Variable names are prefixed with the @ symbol and should have a name made of letters [a-z], numbers [0-9], and underscores. Variable names are case-insensitive, the variable @Ab__11 is the same as @aB__101.

Declaring a Variable

In MSSQL, you muse declare a variable and its type before you may use it. You may also declare an initial value. An uninitialized variable will contain the NULL value until it is assigned.

Statement	Description
DECLARE @var_name data_type;	Create a new local variable of data type and assign the initial value to NULL.
DECLARE @var_name data_type = value;	Create a new local variable of data type and assign the initial value.

Table: MSSQL Declare Statement

Example

Declare two variables, an integer foo, and a variable named 'uuid' with a new UUID in it.

```
DECLARE @foo INTEGER;
DECLARE @uuid VARCHAR(36) = NEWID();
```

---

[164] https://www.sqlite.org/cli.html
[165] https://www.sqlite.org/lang__expr.html#parameters
[166] https://learn.microsoft.com/en-us/sql/t-sql/language-elements/variables-transact-sql?view=sql-server-ver16

Setting a Variable

In addition to being able to set a variable when it is declared, MSSQL Server also allows you to set a variable with the **SET** statement or in an expression in another SQL statement.

Using the SET Statement

To assign a value to an expression, use the **SET** statement.

Table 289: MSSQL Set Statement

Statement	Description
SET @variable = expression;	Set the variable with the expression.

Example

For example, we can set variables with specific values or even with the results of another statement:

```
DECLARE @invoice INTEGER = 12345;
DECLARE @userName VARCHAR(30);
DECLARE @num_live_animals INTEGER;

SET @userName = 'Lex';
SET @num_live_animals = (SELECT count(*)
    FROM animal WHERE death_datetime IS NULL);

SELECT @invoice, @USERNAME, @NUM_LIVE_animals;
```

(No column name)	(No column name)	(No column name)
12345	Lex	7

Setting in an SQL Statement

You may also assign a value to a declared variable by assigning a variable as you calculate an expression in your SQL statement. Use an equal sign after the variable name to assign an expression.

Example

As an example, we will execute a **SELECT** to calculate the total outstanding balances of all owners and then list the owners with a balance and their percentage of the total outstanding.

```
DECLARE @outstanding MONEY;

SELECT @outstanding = SUM(balance) FROM owner;

SELECT last_name, first_name, balance,
    ROUND(balance/@outstanding * 100,0) AS 'Percent'
    FROM owner
    JOIN ownerbalance
    ON owner.owner_id = ownerbalance.owner_id
    WHERE balance <> 0;
```

last_name	first_name	balance	Percent
Smithson	Amy	123.45	26
Greene	Susan	345.98	74

Stored Procedures and Functions

A stored procedure will allow you to save regularly used SQL statements to the database with a custom name. You may use the stored code in your other statements or external programs. There are several benefits to using stored procedures: 1) quicker, 2) easier, and 3) consistency. Stored procedures or user defined functions are implemented by the database providers differently. Please see the sections for each individual database.

MySQL and MariaDB

Stored procedures allow for complex operations in SQL to be stored in the database server and reused. MySQL has complete support for stored procedures.[167]

Setting your Delimiter in the CLI

When creating a stored procedure in the Command Line Interface (CLI), you will need to change the end of statement delimiter. The code in your stored procedure will contain one or more SQL statements, and when you enter the ';' at their end, the database will think you are ending the definition of the stored procedure. To change this behavior, we will execute the DELIMITER statement to temporarily change the end of statement delimiter to something else. In the following example, the end of statement is changed to the string '$$', and then changed back.

---

[167] https://dev.mysql.com/doc/refman/8.4/en/create-procedure.html

Table 292: MySQL Set new End of Statement Delimiter

Statement	Description
DELIMITER string	Set the end of statement delimiter to the supplied string. There is no end of statement (;) because the end of this statement becomes the end of statement.

Example

```
DELIMITER $$
SELECT 1,2,3$$SELECT 4,5,6$$
DELIMITER ;
```

Will display the two recordsets below:

1	2	3
1	2	3

1 row in set (0.000 sec)

4	5	6
4	5	6

1 row in set (0.000 sec)

A Simple Stored Procedure

Here is a simple stored procedure that executes two **SELECT** statements in the veterinarian's office database.

| Statement | | | ──────────────────────── | | CREATE PROCEDURE procedure_name(arguments, ...) BEGIN statements END | Table: MySQL Create Procedure Statement

```
DELIMITER $$
CREATE PROCEDURE Show5()
BEGIN
    SELECT owner_id, last_name, first_name, email
    FROM owner
    WHERE owner_id = 5;

    SELECT name, color, species_id
    FROM animal
```

224

```
    WHERE owner_id = 5
    AND death_datetime IS NULL;
END$$
DELIMITER ;
```

To start a stored procedure executing, we use the **CALL** statement.

Table 295: Call Procedure Statement

Statement
CALL procedure(arguments, ...);

```
CALL show5();
```

Will execute the two **SELECT** statements in the procedure and display these results:

owner_id	last_name	first_name	email
5	Clark	John	johnnyc@notreal.com

```
1 row in set (0.001 sec)
```

name	color	species_id
Penny	Ginger	C
——	——	-
Rosie	Black	C

```
3 rows in set (0.001 sec)
```

```
Query OK, 0 rows affected (0.001 sec)
```

Passing a Value to your Procedure

A better version would be a procedure to show any owner's information. We can define an **IN** variable to collect the owner number from the user and use it in our statements. The procedure variable should not be the same name as an attribute or a table in one of our queries. When we use the variable created in the procedure definition, we do not prefix it with **@** like with other variables.

```
DELIMITER $$
CREATE PROCEDURE ShowOwner(IN own INTEGER)
BEGIN
    SELECT owner_id, last_name, first_name, email
    FROM owner
    WHERE owner_id = own;
```

```
    SELECT name, color, species_id
    FROM animal
    WHERE owner_id = own
    AND death_datetime IS NULL;
END$$
DELIMITER ;
```

The new procedure can be called with an owner number in the parenthesis to display the name, email, and any living animals.

```
call showOwner(1);
```

Will display the following:

owner_id	last_name	first_name	email
1	Smithson	Amy	asmit89@notreal.com

```
1 row in set (0.001 sec)
```

name	color	species_id
Kitty	Ginger	C

```
1 row in set (0.001 sec)
```

```
Query OK, 0 rows affected (0.001 sec)
```

A Procedure to Create a Transaction

Stored procedures are often used to create a uniform way to automate complex inserts and updates. For example, we want to create a procedure to post an owner's payment and update their balance in a single operation.

```
DELIMITER $$

CREATE PROCEDURE postPayment(
    IN payowner INTEGER,
    IN paydatetime DATETIME,
    IN paydescription VARCHAR(50),
    IN payamount DECIMAL)
BEGIN

    START TRANSACTION;

    INSERT INTO payments (payment_uuid, owner_id, payment_datetime,
        description, amount)
```

```
        VALUES
        (UUID(), payowner, paydatetime,
        paydescription, payamount);

    INSERT INTO ownerbalance
        (owner_id, balance) VALUES
        (payowner, payamount * -1)
        ON DUPLICATE KEY UPDATE
        balance = balance - payamount;

    COMMIT;

    SELECT 'Payment posted.';
END$$

DELIMITER ;

CALL postPayment(1, NOW(), 'check 123', 100.00);
```

Returns:

'Payment posted.'
Payment posted.

1 row in set (0.011 sec)

Query OK, 2 rows affected (0.011 sec)

Creating a Stored Function

A stored function is like a stored procedure except that it returns a single value and can be used in any expression. Think of it as a way to automate common calculations or the building of other expressions.

Our veterinarian would like to add a monthly carrying charge to delinquent accounts. They have decided that a monthly charge of 1.5% will be calculated and added to the balance. As a part of this, we can create a function that takes the current balance, adds the charge, and returns the new balance.

```
DELIMITER $$

CREATE FUNCTION calcCarryingCharge(
    IN balance DECIMAL(12,2)
)
RETURNS REAL
BEGIN
    RETURN ROUND(balance * 1.015, 2);
```

```
END$$

DELIMITER ;

SELECT owner_id, last_name, first_name, balance,
    calcCarryingCharge(balance) as NewBalance
    FROM owner
    JOIN ownerbalance
    ON owner.owner_id = ownerbalance.owner_id
    WHERE balance > 0;
```

owner_id	last_name	first_name	balance	NewBalance
1	Smithson	Amy	23.45	23.8
3	Greene	Susan	345.98	351.17
4	Luton	Lex	76.50	77.65

We can also use the function in an **UPDATE** statement to actually add the charge to the current balance.

```
UPDATE ownerbalance
    SET balance = calcCarryingCharge(balance)
    WHERE balance > 0;
```

Listing Stored Procedures and Functions

In MySQL, the 'information_schema' is a special system level database with several tables that store the underlying metadata about our databases. To get a list of stored procedures and functions for a database, we need to query the 'information_schema.routines' table. It contains information about the routines for the entire system.[168]

The following query will show stored procedures and functions. It uses the **DATABASE()** function to get the name of the currently open database.[169]

```
SELECT  routine_schema,
        routine_name,
        routine_type
FROM information_schema.routines
WHERE routine_schema = DATABASE()
ORDER BY routine_name;
```

routine_schema	routine_name	routine_type
vetoffice	addCharge	PROCEDURE

---

[168]https://soft-builder.com/how-to-list-stored-procedures-and-functions-in-mysql-database/
[169]https://dev.mysql.com/doc/refman/8.4/en/information-functions.html#function_database

routine_schema	routine_name	routine_type
vetoffice	calcCarryingCharge	FUNCTION
vetoffice	postPayment	PROCEDURE
vetoffice	Show5	PROCEDURE
vetoffice	ShowOwner	PROCEDURE

Deleting a Stored Procedure or Function

The `DROP PROCEDURE` and `DROP FUNCTION` statements are used to delete a procedure or a function. You will need to drop a procedure or function and recreate it if you want to change how it works.

Table 303: Drop a Stored Procedure or Function

Statement	Description
`DROP PROCEDURE name;`	Delete a stored procedure.
`DROP FUNCTION name;`	Delete a stored function.

SQLite

SQLite does not have the functionality to create stored functions or procedures.

Extensive procedures may be created in a variety of languages that will open databases, create tables, insert and update values, and extract values for you. It is common to do this type of scripting using a language like Python.[170] A brief example of a program that will perform a variety of operations on an SQLite database is listed below.

A common type of security problem with scripting SQL statements is called an SQL Injection Vulnerability. This can occur when an attacker creates a specifically crafted string of data that may cause unwanted embedded SQL to be built into a statement by your program. This may be easily avoided by using parameters in your statement and allowing the database driver to quote any text, automatically.

```
import sqlite3

db = sqlite3.connect('books.sqlite3')

c = db.cursor()

c.execute('CREATE TABLE books (id INTEGER PRIMARY KEY,'
    'title TEXT, author TEXT);')
print(c.rowcount)
```

---

[170]https://docs.python.org/3/library/sqlite3.html

```
dat = {'id': 44, 'title': 'Animal Farm', 'author':'George Orwell'}

c.execute('INSERT INTO books (id, title, author)'
    'VALUES (@id, @title, @author);', dat)
print(c.rowcount)

db.commit()

c.execute('SELECT * FROM books;')
for row in c.fetchall():
    print(row)

db.close()
```

MSSQL Server

MSSQL Server fully supports the use of stored procedures and functions. But like many things, the specific syntax is subtly different.[171]

A Simple Stored Procedure

To create a stored procedure, use the **CREATE PROCEDURE** statement as documented. In this first example, we will create one that has no parameters (values passed into it) and simply executes a **SELECT** statement in the veterinarian's office database.[172]

MSSQL implements the ability to create schemas within a database to contain database objects with owners and permissions. The 'dbo' schema is the default schema when a procedure or function is created and is assumed in the **CREATE** statement.[173]

Table 304: MSSQL Create Procedure Statement

Statement
CREATE PROCEDURE [schema.]procedure_name(arguments, ...) AS BEGIN statements END;

```
CREATE PROCEDURE ShowLiveAnimals
AS
```

[171]https://learn.microsoft.com/en-us/sql/relational-databases/stored-procedures/stored-procedures-database-engine?view=sql-server-ver16

[172]https://learn.microsoft.com/en-us/sql/relational-databases/stored-procedures/create-a-stored-procedure?view=sql-server-ver16

[173]https://learn.microsoft.com/en-us/sql/relational-databases/security/authentication-access/ownership-and-user-schema-separation?view=sql-server-ver16#the-dbo-schema

```
BEGIN
    SELECT last_name, first_name, name, species_id
        FROM animal
        JOIN owner ON animal.owner_id = owner.owner_id
        WHERE death_datetime IS NULL;
END;
```

In MSSQL, a stored procedure is started with the **EXEC** command. If the procedure requires values or arguments passed, then the name is followed by a space and comma separated arguments.[174] In this example, there are no arguments to pass to the procedure.

```
EXEC ShowLiveAnimals;
```

last_name	first_name	name	species_id
Smithson	Amy	Kitty	C
Greene	Susan	Daisy	C
Greene	Susan	Cookie	C
Luton	Lex	Cookie	D
Clark	John	Penny	C
Clark	John	Holly	C
Clark	John	Rosie	C

Passing a Value to your Procedure

To create a procedure that will accept arguments or parameters, we list them in parentheses after the procedure name with their data type. Unlike MySQL, these parameters should follow the naming convention of a variable and should start with an @ sign.

```
CREATE PROCEDURE ShowLiveAnimalsOwner
(
    @owner INTEGER
)
AS
BEGIN
    SELECT last_name, first_name, name, species_id
        FROM animal
        JOIN owner ON animal.owner_id = owner.owner_id
        WHERE owner.owner_id = @owner
        AND death_datetime IS NULL;
END;
```

---

[174]https://learn.microsoft.com/en-us/sql/relational-databases/stored-procedures/execute-a-stored-procedure?view=sql-server-ver16

Now that we have created this procedure, we will execute it and show the living animals for owner number 3.

```
EXEC ShowLiveAnimalsOwner 3
```

last_name	first_name	name	species_id
Greene	Susan	Daisy	C
Greene	Susan	Cookie	C

A Procedure to Create a Transaction

The previous two examples show the basic structure of how to create a stored procedure. Stored procedures are most often used to complete complex database operations and updates. For example, we want to create a procedure to post a charge on an animal and update their owner's balance in a single operation.

```
CREATE PROCEDURE postCharge(
    @animalid INTEGER,
    @datetime DATETIME,
    @description VARCHAR(50),
    @amount DECIMAL(12,2)
)
AS
BEGIN
    DECLARE @ownerid INTEGER;

    BEGIN TRANSACTION;

    SELECT @ownerid = owner_id
        FROM animal
        WHERE animal_id = @animalid;

    INSERT INTO charges (charge_uuid, animal_id, charge_datetime,
        description, amount)
        VALUES
        (NEWID(), @animalid, @datetime,
        @description, @amount);

    UPDATE ownerbalance
        SET balance = balance + @amount
        WHERE owner_id = @ownerid;

    IF (@@ROWCOUNT = 0)
        INSERT INTO ownerbalance
            (owner_id, balance) VALUES
            (@ownerid, @amount);
```

```
    COMMIT;

    SELECT 'Charge posted.';
END;
GO
```

We can now execute the procedure to post a new charge for animal #6 and update the balance for their owner.

```
DECLARE @d DATETIME = GETDATE();
EXEC postCharge 6, @d, 'in office exam', 56.75
```

(No column name)
Charge posted.

Creating a Stored Function

A stored function returns a single value and can be used in an expression. It is a convenient way to automate common calculations.[175] A user defined function may not alter the contents or structure of the database.

Our veterinarian would like to add a monthly carrying charge to delinquent accounts. They have decided that a monthly charge of 1.5% will be calculated and added to the balance. As a part of this, we can create a function that takes the current balance, adds the charge, and returns the new balance.

```
CREATE FUNCTION calcCarryingCharge (
    @balance DECIMAL(12,2)
)
RETURNS DECIMAL(12,2)
AS
BEGIN
    RETURN ROUND(@balance * 1.015, 2);
END;
```

When we created the function above, without a schema, it was added to the default 'dbo' schema. To call this function in a statement, we need to add dbo. before the function name.

```
SELECT owner_id, last_name, first_name, balance,
    dbo.calcCarryingCharge(balance) as NewBalance
    FROM owner
    JOIN ownerbalance
    ON owner.owner_id = ownerbalance.owner_id
    WHERE balance > 0;
```

---

[175]https://learn.microsoft.com/en-us/sql/t-sql/statements/create-function-transact-sql?view=sql-server-ver16

owner_id	last_name	first_name	balance	NewBalance
1	Smithson	Amy	123.45	125.30
3	Greene	Susan	345.98	351.17
4	Luton	Lex	56.75	57.60

Listing Stored Procedures and Functions

MSSQL Server provides a stored procedure to list stored procedures and functions in a schema.[176] In our examples, we have created our procedures and functions in the 'dbo' schema, so we will limit our listing to only include them.

```
EXEC sp_stored_procedures @sp_owner=N'dbo'
```

PROCEDURE_QUALIFIER	PROCEDURE_OWNER	PROCEDURE_NAME	...
vetoffice	dbo	calcCarryingCharge;0	...
vetoffice	dbo	postCharge;1	...
vetoffice	dbo	ShowLiveAnimals;1	...
vetoffice	dbo	ShowLiveAnimalsOwner;1	...

Deleting a Stored Procedure or Function

The `DROP PROCEDURE` and 'DROP FUNCTION' statements are used to delete a procedure or a function. You must first drop a stored routine and recreate it if you want to change it.[177] [178]

Table 310: Drop a Stored Procedure or Function

Statement	Description
`DROP PROCEDURE name;`	Delete a stored procedure.
`DROP FUNCTION name;`	Delete a stored function.

Case

For the case, we will use the GeneralLedger sample database and create stored procedures and functions to create and validate ledger transactions. This case will be in the MSSQL syntax.

---

[176]https://learn.microsoft.com/en-us/sql/relational-databases/system-stored-procedures/sp-stored-procedures-transact-sql?view=sql-server-ver16

[177]https://learn.microsoft.com/en-us/sql/relational-databases/stored-procedures/delete-a-stored-procedure?view=sql-server-ver16

[178]https://learn.microsoft.com/en-us/sql/t-sql/statements/drop-function-transact-sql?view=sql-server-ver16

1) Start a transaction and return the transaction_uuid:

```
CREATE PROCEDURE startTransaction (
    @transdatetime DATETIME,
    @company INTEGER,
    @description VARCHAR(40),
    @transaction VARCHAR(36) OUTPUT
)
AS
BEGIN
    BEGIN TRANSACTION;
    SELECT @transaction = NEWID();

    INSERT INTO ledgertransaction (transaction_uuid,
        transaction_datetime, company_id, description)
        VALUES (@transaction,
        @transdatetime, @company, @description);

    COMMIT;
END;
```

2) Create the procedure to add an account to a transaction. Update amount if account exists on transaction, otherwise insert it. Also update or create an entry in the account balance table.

```
CREATE PROCEDURE addTransactionDetail (
    @transaction VARCHAR(36),
    @account INTEGER,
    @amount DECIMAL(12,2)
)
AS
BEGIN
    BEGIN TRANSACTION;

    DECLARE @company INTEGER;

    SELECT @company = company_id FROM ledgertransaction
        WHERE transaction_uuid = @transaction;

    UPDATE ledgertransactiondetail
        SET amount = amount + @amount
        WHERE transaction_uuid = @transaction
        AND account_id = @account;

    IF (@@ROWCOUNT = 0)
        INSERT INTO ledgertransactiondetail
                (transaction_uuid, account_id, amount)
```

```
                VALUES (@transaction, @account, @amount);

        UPDATE accountbalance
            SET balance = balance + @amount
            WHERE company_id = @company
            AND account_id = @account;

        IF (@@ROWCOUNT = 0)
            INSERT INTO accountbalance
                    (company_id, account_id, balance)
                    VALUES (@company, @account, @amount);

        COMMIT;
END;
```

3) Create a function to total a transaction's debits and credits and return a message stating if the transaction is in balance or not.

```
CREATE FUNCTION testTransaction (
    @transaction VARCHAR(36)
)
RETURNS VARCHAR(50)
AS
BEGIN
    DECLARE @balance DECIMAL(12,2);
    DECLARE @message VARCHAR(40);
    SELECT @balance = SUM(amount) FROM ledgertransactiondetail
        WHERE transaction_uuid = @transaction;
    IF (@balance=0)
        SET @message = 'Transaction is in balance.';
    ELSE
        SET @message = CONCAT_WS(' ',
                'Transaction is out of balance by',
                @balance, '.');
    RETURN @message;
END;
```

5) Use the procedures and functions to post the following ledger transaction:

We are making our initial stock purchase of $1000 into company #2 right now. Our contribution will be $750 in cash and $250 in inventory into the company.

```
DECLARE @d DATETIME = GETDATE();
DECLARE @id VARCHAR(36);
EXEC startTransaction  @d, 2, 'stock purchase', @id OUTPUT;
EXEC addTransactionDetail @id, 100, 750;
EXEC addTransactionDetail @id, 190, 250;
SELECT dbo.testTransaction( @id );
```

```
EXEC addTransactionDetail @id, 300, -1000;
SELECT dbo.testTransaction( @id );
```

(No column name)
Transaction is out of balance by 1000.00 .

(No column name)
Transaction is in balance.

Exercises

Using the Toy Store Order sample database answer the following.

1. Create a stored procedure that will start a new order. It needs to create an order_header with a unique ID with a total of zero.

2. Create a stored procedure that will add an item with price and quantity to an order.

3. Create another procedure to add an item and quantity to an order. Retrieve the current price from the item table and then execute/call the stored procedure above to actually perform the update.

4. Create a function that will accept item_id and discount percent as arguments and return the sale price.

This page intentionally left blank.

Appendix A – Sample SQL Databases

There are several sample databases that have been created for use as examples and for exercises in the chapters.

GeneralLedger – Simplified Accounting Transactions

The "GeneralLedger" database is a very simple multi-company general ledger database that uses the same chart of accounts for each company.

In GeneralLedger:

- There are account types like asset, liability, income, and others.
- An account has one account type.
- A company may have several accounts and an account may be used by many companies.
- Each company and account combination will have a balance.
- Ledger transactions will belong to one company and may post into many accounts for that company.
- To keep debits (+) and credits (-) in balance, a ledger transaction's detail may only post to an account once and the sum of the detail amounts must be zero.

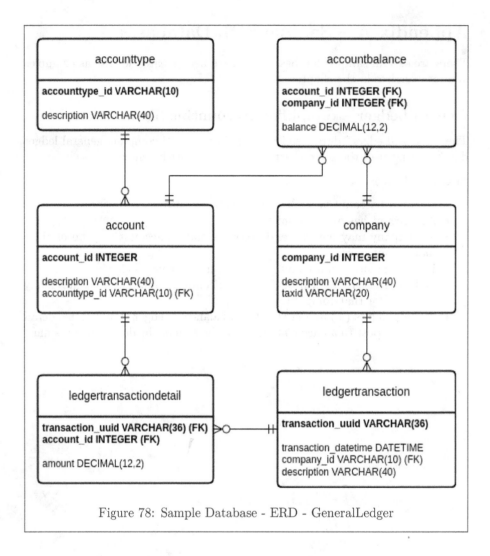

Figure 78: Sample Database - ERD - GeneralLedger

MediaCollection – Movies and Albums

The "MediaCollection" database allows me keep track of the movies and albums in my collection.

In MediaCollection:

- A song must have one artist.
- An artist may have zero or more songs.
- An artist may have zero or more albums of songs.
- An album must have one or more songs on it, and it must have an artist.
- A song may be on zero or more albums.
- A studio may create multiple movies and a movie has one studio.

- An artist may direct zero or more movies, and a movie must be directed by one artist.

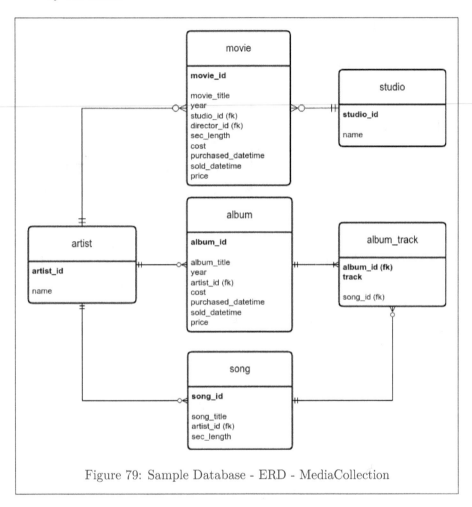

Figure 79: Sample Database - ERD - MediaCollection

ToyStoreOrder – A Toy Store and Orders

The "ToyStoreOrder" database is a bit more complex than the first two. It tracks the relationships between customers and what they have purchased and when. It also has data about who we order individual items from.

In ToyStoreOrder:

- An item may exist on several orders.
- A customer may have several orders.
- An order must have at least one item associated.
- A vendor supplies several items and an item is provided by one vendor.

- A customer may have invoices sent to another customer (bill to).

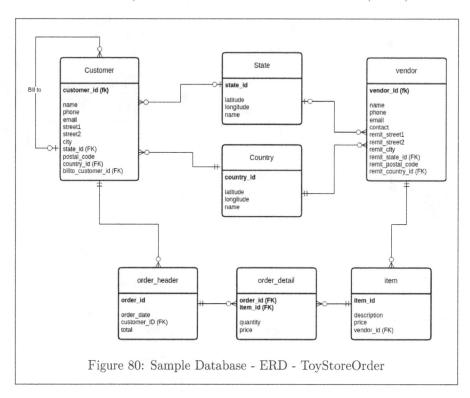

Figure 80: Sample Database - ERD - ToyStoreOrder

VetOffice - Veterinarian's Office to Track Animals

The database "VetOffice" is a simple database used by a veterinarian's office to keep track of owners, their pets, charges and payments.

In VetOffice:

- An animal has one gender, one owner, and belongs to one species.
- An animal is assumed to be alive if it does not have a death date.
- A gender, species, or owner may have zero or more associated animals.
- An owner may have zero or more animals.
- The office will perform services or charge for supplies or products to an animal. This way we can track what has been done for a specific animal.
- An owner will make payments to cover the balance of charges for one or more animal.
- If an owner has had charges and/or payments, a balance record with their current balance will be maintained.

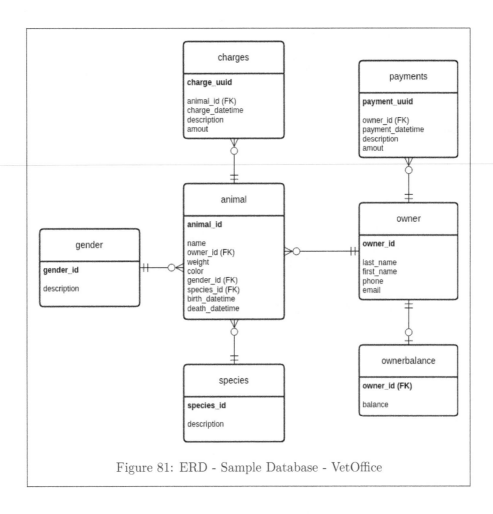

Figure 81: ERD - Sample Database - VetOffice

This page intentionally left blank.

Index